The Corona Generation

Coming of Age in a Crisis

The Corona Generation

Coming of Age in a Crisis

Jennie Bristow and Emma Gilland

Winchester, UK
Washington, USA

JOHN HUNT PUBLISHING

First published by Zero Books, 2021
Zero Books is an imprint of John Hunt Publishing Ltd., No. 3 East St., Alresford,
Hampshire SO24 9EE, UK
office@jhpbooks.com
www.johnhuntpublishing.com
www.zero-books.net

For distributor details and how to order please visit the 'Ordering' section on our website.

Text copyright: Jennie Bristow 2020

ISBN: 978 1 78904 693 9
978 1 78904 694 6 (ebook)
Library of Congress Control Number: 2020942479

A CIP catalogue record for this book is available from the British Library.

Design: Stuart Davies

UK: Printed and bound by CPI Group (UK) Ltd, Croydon, CR0 4YY
Printed in North America by CPI GPS partners

We operate a distinctive and ethical publishing philosophy in
all areas of our business, from our global network of authors to
production and worldwide distribution.

Contents

Acknowledgements 1

Chapter 1: Coming of age in a crisis 3

Chapter 2: Fear goes viral 16

Chapter 3: Virtual intimacies 35

Chapter 4: The adult world retreats 53

Chapter 5: Lockdown labelling 70

Chapter 6: Moving on 84

Endnotes: 90

Acknowledgements

There are many people to thank for supporting us in writing *The Corona Generation*, and making the process of pursuing this particular 'lockdown project' less lonely and isolating than it otherwise would have been. First and foremost, our family: Tony, for encouraging us along the way and commenting on drafts and ideas, and Annia, for stoically ploughing through her schoolwork, providing the hugs, and putting up with the constant Covid conversations. Thank you both: we love you very much.

A big thank you goes to friends and acquaintances who talked to us about their experiences of the crisis, and provided their reflections. Some of these are quoted in the book. Many more helped us to interpret the moment, illustrating where we were not alone in our own feelings about lockdown and where others had a different take on things. We could not have written this without your insights.

Thanks to those who took the time to read and comment on drafts: in particular, Frank, Ellie, Kate, Rachel, Abigail, Anwesa, Charlotte, Kath, and Steve. Thanks also to the Academy of Ideas Parents' Forum and the Generations Network for providing a space for us to discuss our ideas as we were developing them. We are hugely grateful to the team at Zero Books for their support for this project, from commissioning through production – it has been wonderful to work with you.

During lockdown, a big absence in our lives was physical contact with our extended family and friends – grandparents, aunts, uncles, cousins, and lifelong friends who live too far away to be casually 'bumped into' on the permitted daily walks. As we write these acknowledgements, it has been 4 months since we have seen any of them 'in real life', and that has been hard. Back in January, we celebrated the Bristow grandparents' Golden

Wedding Anniversary, with two large, intergenerational parties involving no social distancing whatsoever. That memory, of the time 'Before Corona', helped to carry us through the isolating months that followed.

We dedicate this book to the Class of 2020.

Chapter 1

Coming of age in a crisis

My daughter Emma turned 16 in June 2020. Until mid-March, she had been dutifully swotting for her GCSEs – the public exams sat by students across England, Wales, and Northern Ireland in the summer of the school Year 11. Then, she wasn't.

Historically, GCSE exams have marked the end of compulsory secondary school, and an important milestone in growing up. Up and down Britain, 15-16-year-olds participate in a long-established ritual – the cramming, the drama, the intensity of sweating through paper after paper in a stuffy school hall or gym. In August, the newspapers capture familiar images of students congregating at their schools to rip open their results envelopes – some laughing and waving their top grades, some crying and complaining. It's a Thing.

It's not just 'Their Thing', either. For students across the Western world in the demographic known as 'Generation Z', educational achievements and ceremonies play the role of established rites of passage on the journey to adulthood. High school and university graduation ceremonies, with their paraphernalia of mortar-board caps and gowns, year books, and proms, signify both individual academic achievement and a more collective, peer group identity. But for the 'Class of 2020' – encompassing students aged between 15 and 22, depending on which country they live in and the stage of their educational journey – the Thing that has for so long symbolized entry to the next phase of life suddenly became Nothing. One day, school and college students were revving to the mantra of 'these grades will determine the rest of your life'; the next, they were suspended mid-flight as nations rapidly closed their schools and colleges, and put their populations into lockdown.

Gracie, a college senior in the US, had been looking forward to the traditional send-off: 'to stay up the whole night, watch the sunrise and then nearly die through graduation'. Instead:

> I sat at home with my friends because we weren't allowed to go anywhere. We painted our nails, had some wine then went to bed – in the morning I packed my stuff and went... My friends and I were talking about how when we have kids, we are going to be those parents who are obsessed with graduation because we didn't get to have one and I think that will affect our generation, and make us value our college or high school experience in a different way. Because we lost some of it.

On its own, the loss of a graduation ceremony might not seem like a big deal. But it wasn't the loss of the day itself that bothered the young people whom we talked to, so much as the symbolism of the moment.

Some felt that they had been summarily rejected from the institutions that had shaped their lives for several years. 'People wanted the chance to prove themselves, the cheesy last day, the prom, the results day – and they'd never get it,' said Maria, 16. 'All in all I felt cheated out of the end of my school career.' Maria is going on to sixth-form college in September. She described how, during the week when exam cancellation and school closures were announced, 'no-one knew how to react or what to expect – I don't think many people even picked up a pen'; and recalled the uncertainty and confusion of her last school day:

> Something that was supposed to happen in June was happening in mid-March and you could feel the attitude in the air just wasn't the same. The school Assembly was hastily thrown together with a few teachers getting mildly choked up during half-hearted speeches. Afterwards we

were herded, like little sheep, to the basketball courts at the bottom of the school, and told that we had an allotted half hour to sign shirts and say our goodbyes. After that they basically evicted us from the school. After all, we weren't important to them anymore, we didn't have GCSEs to pass, we didn't have anything to learn from them. So we left.

Sitting at home that night I don't think anything felt real – it didn't for anyone. When I said goodbye to people that day it was in the knowledge that I wouldn't see many of them, including my friends, for another five months and possibly never again.

At Emma's school, staff made a valiant effort to make their last day special, organizing a free 'Leavers' Lunch' in the canteen and a party atmosphere, with yearbook-style photos published in the school newsletter. One of my local friends, another Year 11 mum whose garden backs onto the school field, posted on Facebook that she could hear the kids cheering. I sat in my own garden, looking at Facebook, and cried.

Then I pulled myself together, and decided to write this book.

I decided to write this book for three reasons. First, as a sociologist focused on the study of generations, it was immediately apparent that what UK prime minister Boris Johnson described as 'the worst public health crisis for a generation'[1] would be epoch-defining. As the international response to the pandemic unfolded, following a peculiarly uniform path of lockdowns, school closures, and grinding economies to a sudden halt, it was also clear that while the crisis would have a major impact on everybody, it would have particular significance for the 'Corona generation': the young people coming of age at this time. This is not to say that it will be worse for them than for older people – it is that, because of where they are in the life course, the experience will be formative.

Linking to my previous work on generational labelling and conflict, the book explores the significance of this particular moment for young people's encounters with the world around them. I suggest that this moment is likely to provoke the emergence of a distinctive generational consciousness: it will mark these kids for life. But I also caution against seeing this as the end of their world. Rather, it is a new chapter in a story of economic and institutional crisis that was already unfolding, and one in which young people will have a significant role in shaping going forwards. Hence the 'Corona generation' – named for a crown, not a virus; a social shock, not a natural disease.

The second motivation was that, as an educator, I found myself deeply disturbed by the speed with which schools and universities across the world were forced to close their doors, and by the apparent nonchalance about when they might admit their students again. The justification for these closures was a narrow focus on infection control, with little consideration given to the reasons why, *particularly* during a national crisis, educational institutions have a vital role to play in helping to steer young people through difficult times.

School is the place where the adult world meets the child world, where social norms and values are communicated across the generations, and also where children gain the sense of belonging to a generation of their peers. In giving children access to their society's cultural heritage, education takes children outside the febrile tensions of their daily existence and gives them a wider, deeper sense of perspective on the human condition, and the tools to know and understand life's mysteries. Yet in the rush to close schools and the reluctance to reopen them, the educational and moral purpose of schooling has been remarkably lightly held.

'Schoolwork' was quickly reduced to the project of following the curriculum online, with parents charged with getting their kids through their daily tasks, and teachers reduced to disembodied instruction-and-feedback facilitators. All the things that were previously communicated to young people about the importance of attending school, engaging in their lessons, and working hard for their exams were indefinitely suspended. As I write, it is by no means certain that, even after lockdown, young people will be 'going back to school' in a meaningful sense. This raises some wider questions about the Corona Generation's encounter with education, and with the institutions of adult society.

The third motivation for the book was that, as a mother of two teenage girls, I needed to find some way of helping them to make sense of this moment; and find something for them to do. One of the most peculiar features of the response to the pandemic is that it has mobilized populations around the imperative of staying indoors, and away from each other. Teenagers were not only expelled from the educational world; they were effectively barred from engaging in a wider social response to the unfolding social and economic crisis.

My initial hope was that the pupils suddenly liberated from school by the cancellation of exams could be brought into a constructive response to the problem, by working or volunteering to help in the community. But the strictures of lockdown swiftly made this *verboten* for kids under 18, for whom the message was that the best way they could serve their country was by sitting on their collective arse. Rather than engage healthy young people in the difficult questions about what should be done, we locked them in a physical and intellectual quarantine, and told them to put up and shut up.

This might all be very unpleasant – but is it the end of the world? We are living through a pandemic, after all, in which difficult decisions have to be made and health is prioritized over happiness. The kind of traumatic social events that have historically forced generations to develop a distinctive sense of themselves have been wars, in which millions of young men were killed before their lives had even started. To follow the wartime analogies invoked by political leaders and the Queen of England during the pandemic as they have sought to justify the hardships wrought on their populations, it is ridiculous to suggest that being stuck in front of a screen for a few weeks is comparable to the experience of children evacuated to the countryside in Britain during the Second World War – or to those across Europe, who faced far worse fates. The mother of one of my friends, now in her 80s, was evacuated to Canada with her mother for the duration of the war: on the crossing, the ship in front of them was blown up.

One remarkable feature of Covid-19 is that, as a disease, it generally spares the young. Unlike the killing fields of the Somme or Vietnam, most kids will come out of all this physically and mentally intact, with a future that will be theirs to shape. But what meaning will they draw from this experience? What impact will the conditioned impotence and atomization of lockdown have on how our children see their society, and how they see themselves? That is the question at the heart of this book.

Thinking about generations

Emma and I have written this book together (although I take responsibility for any mistakes). Through Emma's accounts, and those she has gained from friends and acquaintances in the UK and North America, we illustrate how the Covid-19 crisis was playing out in the thoughts of some young people in the early stages of lockdown (March and April 2020).[2] We make no claim to describing or understanding the wider experience of kids across the UK, let alone the world, who are affected by this crisis. Young people's experience of the pandemic and its aftermath, like their experience of life before, is powerfully framed by social class, ethnicity, gender, and their geographical location – arguably far more so than by their birth cohort. Those experiences will require proper documentation, reflection, and analysis of the kind that it is impossible to do when writing in the moment. As a friend of mine wryly remarked at the start of the UK's lockdown, 'well, this is an interesting social experiment which will keep sociologists busy for decades to come'.

It is also important to stress that individuals – within all generations – have experienced lockdown differently. Some have rather enjoyed the break from the rat-race, continuing to earn their salaries in a more relaxed 'WFH' ('Working from Home') environment, while others find the experience isolating and practically very difficult; some are distraught by the prospect of cuts in their pay and the loss of their jobs, while others have been working harder than ever in 'key worker' jobs while the pandemic was raging, and are resentful when people whinge about being bored. Some kids may have gained a sense of liberation and purpose by not being at school; some may have experienced enforced isolation from their peers as a massive relief. As C. Wright Mills famously observed in his classic 1950s text *The Sociological Imagination*[3], life is experienced personally, not sociologically. The universal experience of living through a pandemic is mediated by individuals' own circumstances and outlook: we might all be 'in it together', but 'it' has different meanings for each of us.

So this book is not an academic study, or some kind of treatise designed to predict the generational impact of the pandemic. As I have discussed in my previous work, the cultural and political obsession with generations has often been profoundly unhelpful in understanding both individual experience and social change, as it tends to promote a deterministic, generalizing, and divisive narrative of 'generationalism' – a way of thinking that presents social, economic, and political problems through the distorting prism of simplified generational differences.[4] Rather, this book is a reflection on generational consciousness: and particularly, the symbolic context that frames young people's experience of

9

coming of age in a crisis.

Generations can best be understood as powerful 'concepts of existence'[5] which embody the experience of history in those who come of age during moments of social change and crisis. Attempts to understand how 'social generations' are forged have focused on the significance of what June Edmunds and Bryan S. Turner describe as 'traumatic events'.[6] People coming of age in periods of accelerated social change develop a distinct perspective, arising from the fraught encounter between the world as it was and the world as it is.

Suggesting that coronavirus 'could be Generation Z's 9/11', psychology professor and generation theorist Jean Twenge describes a day in early March where 'everything still seemed pretty normal' apart from the newsfeed on her phone, which was announcing the imminent outbreak of the Covid-19 pandemic. 'I was reminded of Sept. 10, 2001 – the day before everything changed the last time,' she writes. 'Except: In many ways, the coronavirus outbreak is bigger than 9/11.' Twenge continues:

We don't know yet how this will play out, but the coronavirus outbreak could become the biggest and most impactful cultural event of our lifetime. Neither 9/11 nor the Great Recession so profoundly altered as many aspects of day-to-day life in such a short period of time the way the coronavirus has affected schools, work, travel, entertainment and shopping. Plus, 9/11 and the recession didn't have as direct an impact on so many people around the world. The outbreak and our reactions to it are not a lone event – they intersect with the trends of the past and will have an impact on the future of many people, especially the generation I call iGen – those born after 1995.[7]

As Twenge suggests, the mediation between the past, present, and future lies at the heart of generational consciousness – and will be starkly experienced by the generation whose coming of age is marked by the distinction between life 'Before Corona' and 'After Corona'.

Understanding the role of social shocks in forging a generation's sense of itself, and its relation to wider society, follows a well-established, though often contested, sociological theory developed in the 1920s by the Hungarian sociologist Karl Mannheim. In his influential essay 'The Problem of Generations', Mannheim theorized that generational consciousness comes from the interaction between cohorts on the cusp of adulthood, and wider social events and cultural forces. During periods of accelerated social change, the past and present collide, creating a schism between the way things were and the way things are. This is what gives members of a generation a sense of fellow-feeling with others of a similar age, and a sense of distinction from older or younger generations.

Mannheim argued that consciousness, in terms of the possibility of 'really questioning and reflecting on things', emerges around the age of 17, 'at the point where personal experimentation with life begins'. It is this emergence of a reflective individual, active in society, that gives youth both the 'freshness' of its contact with society, and its dynamic relationship with cultural renewal:

> The 'up-to-dateness' of youth therefore consists in their being closer to the 'present' problems...and in the fact that they are dramatically aware of a process of destabilization and take sides in it. All this while, the older generation cling to the reorientation that had been the drama of *their* youth.[8]

While everyone's world has been rocked by the Covid-19 crisis, the destabilization experienced by young people is particularly intense. It comes at a time when they are just beginning to discover themselves, following a path into adulthood that, for all it has never been smooth, has been laid down since their birth in a world they are beginning to discover but do not yet truly know. The smashing of this path, and the uncertain social and economic future that lies ahead, is now their reality. While older generations seek to understand times of crisis by drawing on their experience of previous social shocks, the young have no basis for such comparisons, and are forced to make meaning of the experience simply through living it.

The popular 'generation labels' we have today have stuck because they capture something real – the shift between old and new worlds, brought about by traumatic historical events. That is why we have the 'Generation of 1914', symbolically marked by the trauma of the First World War; the 'Greatest Generation', symbolically elevated by the victory against fascism; the 'Baby Boomers', symbolically spaced out by the cultural upheavals of the Sixties; and the 'Millennials', coming of age in the aftermath of the terror attacks of 9/11. Despite their widespread use, these labels reflect a very particular set of ideas about the generations with which they are associated – generally speaking to a middle-class cultural sensibility, forged in early adulthood, which later comes to be associated with the *Zeitgeist*.

As such, the labels also conjure up moments in history. As Shaun Scott writes in *Millennials and the Moments That Made Us*, the descriptor 'Millennial' is not only a 'noun that refers to an age cohort':

> It is also an adjective that refers to a historical situation defined by the technology, politics, and pop culture of the 21st century. One can speak of 'Millennials' as a group, and also refer to a 'millennial' era that previous generations are also living through. Not everybody is a Millennial, but we're all passing through a millennial moment in history.[9]

Scott notes that those who passed through the 'millennial

moment' at the point where they were coming of age have a particular, formative experience of this period. How they make sense of and express that experience then gains significance as they go on to write the next chapter in history. For example, the historian Robert Wohl writes of the common 'conscious[ness] of generational unity' that distinguished the interwar period from 'any era before or afterwards'. The intellectuals of the 'Generation of 1914' saw themselves as 'wanderers between two worlds' – a time of great crisis, bringing an urgent sense of destruction but, also, renewal.[10]

The Corona Generation, too, will find itself wandering between two symbolic universes – between the norms and ideas that provided structure and meaning to Life Before Corona, and those that come to shape Life After Corona. We can hope that the privations of lockdown will be temporary – school will start up again, kids will be able to see their friends again, the parties can resume, and they will begin the next stage of their lives. Although they will never get back the Big Moments they have missed, there will be many others still to come. But the cavalier way in which adult society has suspended its central responsibility to guide and educate young people through periods of crisis will have a significant symbolic effect. In this sense, this book is as much about how adults have come to think about young people as it is about how the Corona Generation might come to think about itself.

Emma's lockdown reflections: The suspension of normal life

For me, the cancellation of exams was a huge deal. The work that had been put in seemed worthless and the activities which dominated my time were cancelled. My evenings, and now days, have turned into a loose end. The last few days have been a new concept of time; as days are longer than before, it leaves us to wonder how long this particularly unstable structure will last and what the days ahead will be filled with – most likely to be tedious tasks and useless boredom.

Boredom and independence are often considered two fundamentals of growing up, but being quarantined with your parents strips away your independence and hits you with boredom, in a new intensified way. For many young people, the restrictions take them back years into their childhood, as parties and school are cancelled, we are rid of all socializing outside the walls of our home. Despite our complaints about school, it provides an escape from the control of parents and bickering with siblings, to be with people you choose and can relate to, with the tedious distractions and lessons keeping you somewhat entertained and distracted, away from the uncertainty of adolescence.

Lack of distraction – that's the biggest hole. With seven extra hours in the day, you need the distraction of everyday life the most, where there is no need to think about yourself, your flaws and the future as you are wrapped up in teenage drama, a happy escape. But this has gone, and it has left a lot of us realizing how lonely and repetitive life really is – we need the walls of school, the voices and repressed laughter, this helps us muddle through our lives. This excitement of the ordinary can't be replaced by Netflix and Instagram, despite what many of us thought. It is remarkable that we stayed as calm as we have when locked in our houses, showing the huge effect on our views and priorities as the fear of infection has become a much greater issue; we are prepared to suffer the mundane to prevent an overwhelming peak.

Globally it seems that for many there has been a mature response to the coronavirus as everyone, even the younger generation, has missed out on something due to the lockdown procedures. Exams, holidays, or sports; something is now missing from people's lives which they had planned for and were excited by, their motivation and drive. However, despite the sense of loss, everyone is moving on, trying to get through and help however they can. Despite the limit to what we can do, the sense of community has grown. To me this is quite impressive, as it shows some selflessness which hadn't been seen in many people before, as they take the sacrifice and use the time in a different way, trying to focus on the bigger picture.

The national movement to fight coronavirus has been refreshing for many of us as it is a break from our own identity politics. As many have phrased it, 'we are living through a future history question' – living in a moment quite different, frightening yet extraordinary. Although there is more time to reflect on ourselves, we are currently engulfed by the global, political, and community affairs as we try to fight the pandemic. Some young people are more involved than others, but we are all talking about it. We are no longer obsessing with fragile relationships but more on the world around us. However, in saying this, many people are more focused on the effects closer to them, which is reasonable enough, but neglecting the bigger picture, such as the issues of unemployment and lack of liberty.

The fact that many of us believed we should isolate to help reduce deaths and pressures on the health service is hugely positive, but we are not weighing up the effects on many of the wider community like the independent business owners, the recently unemployed, and the completely isolated, as many people are living in misery alone and with their lives in turmoil while we are trying to save the lives of others. This provides a huge question about priorities, not only of the government but our own beliefs. The pandemic has brought an additional sense of independence as we are having to deal with every situation alone, mostly isolated from those we would normally talk to – especially when dealing with school as the work has to be done independently of the teacher, so we are having to puzzle it through, more self-sufficiently than before.

Chapter 2

Fear goes viral

The dominant metaphor of Covid-19 has been the imperative to 'Keep the R below 1'. 'R' refers to the virus's reproduction number; the justification for all social distancing measures has been to construct an environment in which each infected person, statistically, will infect fewer than one other person, thereby stopping the infection from spreading exponentially. For all societies in lockdown, the imperative of keeping the R below 1 has meant keeping physically apart from anyone outside of your immediate household.

The sudden contraction of social contact has had an abrupt impact on teenagers and young people, for whom their current life stage has been defined as gradually going beyond the boundaries of childhood. Interrupting transmission of the virus has meant, for them, interrupting a whole train of norms and aspirations to do with growing up – getting to know themselves through forging relationships with others. Although the young people we talked to were confident that these interactions would come back, and hopeful that they would matter more than ever, this rupture will cast a long shadow – not so much because of the lockdown itself, but for the manner in which it has been justified.

At the time of writing, debate continues about the extent to which children are susceptible to contracting the virus, or passing it on, and about the effectiveness of school closures as an infection control strategy with this particular disease. Yet even if locking up the kids turns out to have been a sensible practical move, there are some significant symbolic consequences to the presentation of young people as dangerous spreaders of a deadly disease that they may not have, or may not be aware that they have. The depiction of young people as viral 'super-spreaders' – troublesome, unwitting germs on legs – marshals a narrative of fear and suspicion *about* them, in place of a calm discussion *with* them.

Infection and intimacy – the prequel

One evening, early in the pandemic, a friend and I were reminiscing about AIDS. This terrifying new disease came on the scene in the late 1980s, when we were in our early teens; it gripped our imaginative coming of age and overshadowed our early sexual experiences. The messages promoted then foreshadowed the public health warnings about Covid-19 – this is new, there is no cure, it is spreading, anyone can get it, and anyone can transmit it. The infamous 'iceberg' and 'tombstone' adverts[1] produced by the British government in 1987 hammered home the warning 'Don't die of ignorance': what would protect us from this disease was being afraid of it, and acting upon that fear in the conduct of our sexual relationships.

The generational impact of AIDS was huge. In Western societies, it was particularly significant, of course, for young gay men – the community ravaged by this dreadful disease. As Perry N. Halkitis argues in *The AIDS Generation: Stories of Survival and Resilience*, for this group 'the HIV/AIDS epidemic was a formative experience in fear, hardship, and loss'.[2] But even among the young heterosexual population, where, it turned out, the disease would have a much more limited spread, fear of the unknown provoked a simultaneous generational unity and estrangement – from older generations, and from each other.

Because AIDS was a new disease that was transmitted through sexual intercourse, public health messaging was targeted at young people, on the assumption that the oldies were mainly having sex with their lifelong, pre-infection partner. The big danger, we were instructed, was so-called 'casual sex' – sleeping around meant that you were more likely both to contract the virus, and to pass it on. This was a particular problem because some people would be 'asymptomatic' carriers, and might therefore spread the infection without knowing they were doing it. We were encouraged to think of every particular sexual encounter as a potential chain of infection; you are not only sleeping with that person, but with every person they have slept with before. If you had to have sex, it was imperative to use a 'barrier method' (a condom), but be aware that these might split, leaving you exposed to not only the age-old terror of accidental pregnancy, but becoming infected with AIDS or passing it on to your partner.

It was bloody terrifying. Government campaigns, teen magazines, and sessions organized in schools all sang to the same hymn sheet, and the loss of our virginity came sheathed in fear. We were vocally resentful towards our elders, for having enjoyed what we imagined to be a blissfully innocent encounter with 'free love' (we rarely considered the relative unavailability of abortion and contraception when *they* were coming of age, nor the powerful social conventions that frowned upon sex outside of marriage). And we were grievously suspicious of members of our own generation, to whom we couldn't get too close in case they might accidentally kill us.

We eventually got over it – until talking to my friend, the only times I have thought about AIDS in recent years have been in giving lectures about the sociology of public health, and showing the 'tombstone' ad to students who find it both horrifying and hilarious. But these things leave a mark. For those coming of age during the Covid-19 pandemic, the fear is no less acute than that promoted through the AIDS crisis; and the consequences of the campaign have been far wider reaching – framing not just their sex lives, but their everyday encounters.

The AIDS campaign slogan 'Don't die of ignorance' implied a clear link between fear and behaviour. Clearly, simply knowing about AIDS was not a protection against contracting the disease;

knowledge had to lead to a decision to use a condom, or not to have sex at all. So it was a particular *kind* of knowledge, which emphasized the potential threat of this novel, untreatable, asymptomatically-transmitted virus to young people embarking on sexual adventures. As social scientists have observed, posed in this way, the public-health messaging around AIDS chimed with a pre-existing conservative morality, which saw both gay sex and casual sex as a problem, and fear of AIDS as a way of promoting this moral message through the language and imagery of fear.[3]

The metaphorical dimension of AIDS would in many ways set the script for the wider 'social distancing' messages of the Covid-19 pandemic.

Bringing the threat home

When Emma and her friends described how they felt during the week beginning 16 March, when exam cancellations, school closures, and household lockdown measures were announced in quick succession, a couple of phrases recurred. One was that 'it felt like a dream' – the shift from set-in-stone assessment timetables to a soupy uncertainty, in which teachers and parents were unable to give any guidance on what might happen next until the government had issued its latest press briefing. They also talked of how, even by that point, Covid-19 seemed like a 'distant' threat: the 'world was being shaped by the virus', but it had little connection to their actual lives. 'People loved the drama of the situation,' wrote Maria. 'Although people did wish for the school to be closed, this was more for want of time off, and less to do with concern for fellow students.'

What was it that made the threat of Covid-19 seem real to British teenagers? Fortunately, for most of them it was not that they began to fall ill – nor, in those early days, did their elderly relatives. My daughters' school was associated with a positive case of Covid-19 quite early on – the local media reported on

3 March that 'a number of students had been in contact with Kent's first victim of the deadly virus', who turned out to be the father of two of the pupils, and recovered well.[4] But the school's response was calm: the affected family self-isolated, and the school carried on with advice on handwashing, hygiene, and being aware of symptoms, while riding the dramatic chatter of pupils and parents.

The virus was here in our midst, but the threat hovered at a higher level: charts showing its grim march through Italy and Continental Europe, on other people in other places. And even 2 months later, as we sat in our homes reeling from the UK's daily death toll, it all seemed quite abstract.

To be clear: this is not to say that Covid-19 itself is in any way 'unreal'. Members of the Corona Generation have lost loved ones to this virus – some of whom will be old and frail, others who may be younger and previously healthy. Many of my own friends have been ill with Covid-19, and friends of friends have died. When confronted with a new and deadly disease, it is surely right that societies take preventative measures to minimize its impact, and this necessarily means that awareness of the danger runs ahead of most people's actual experience.

But considering the pandemic's potential impact on generational *consciousness* means considering not just the biological existence of the disease, but the symbolic response to the threat it poses. With regard to the Corona Generation, arguably the most striking has been the pathologization of the youthful, healthy body.

From the start, it has been widely recognized that otherwise healthy young people are statistically far less likely to become seriously ill from Covid-19 than older people or those with underlying health conditions. This was perceived as a good thing: not because the lives of healthy young people are worth more than those of sick or older people, but because a disease that attacks young healthy bodies is likely to have more devastating consequences all round. Health officials in the UK initially took care to stress that children and young adults should not be too anxious about the effect of the virus on themselves, but should be aware of the dangers that the infection might pose to others in their families or communities. This was not just an accurate reflection of the available scientific evidence – it was motivated by a concern to limit unwarranted anxiety among parents and young people, and to encourage healthy, lower-risk people to keep the show on the road, by working and caring for those who needed to be protected from exposure to the virus.

Yet as the tide of fear rose, and with it demands for governments to take drastic actions to 'stop' the virus, the Covid-19 narrative changed from emphasizing young people's relative safety to stressing the danger the virus could pose to them personally, and above all, the danger they could pose to others by being 'asymptomatic carriers'. This message was starkly put on 20 March, when Tedros Adhanom Ghebreyesus, Director General of the World Health Organization (WHO), warned in a virtual press conference:

Although older people are hardest hit, younger people are not spared. Data from many countries clearly show that people under 50 make up a significant proportion of patients requiring hospitalisation.

Today I have a message for young people: You are not invincible, this virus could put you in hospital for weeks or even kill you. Even if you don't get sick the choices you make about where you go could be the difference between life and death for someone else.[5]

The WHO's warning was quickly adopted by governments around the world. In particular, the danger posed by kids as potential 'asymptomatic carriers' became the justification for keeping schools closed and children shut in their homes.

For 6 weeks in Spain, kids were not permitted to go outside at all, prompting Ada Colau, Barcelona's mayor, to issue an impassioned Facebook plea to the government: 'Wait no more: Free our children!'[6]

What changed? When it comes to the age profile of Covid-19, the statistics have been remarkably stable. Despite some tragic individual cases, young people are far less likely to become extremely ill or die from the virus than other age groups. In late April, the Swiss health ministry concluded that scientific evidence showed that young children did not transmit the virus, leading to a poignant BBC News headline, 'Coronavirus: Switzerland says young children can hug grandparents'.[7] But whatever scientific evidence tells us about the extent to which children and young adults are asymptomatic carriers and transmitters of the virus, the global decision to clamp down on kids had a more pragmatic motivation.

Pre-lockdown, claims that young adults were persisting in 'irresponsible' behaviour by continuing to socialize in bars and restaurants were rife. There was a sense that young people were shrugging off concerns about the virus, and carrying on as though nothing had changed. And indeed, many of those whom I talked to about Covid-19 until mid-March weren't in a panic; they seemed almost nonchalant about the endless media coverage, and frustrated with the relentless gush of bad news. But the rush to frame this as a problem of young people's mentality – that they weren't scared enough, and they weren't prepared to sacrifice their social lives – misses some important nuances.

In an astute blog post on *Social Science Space* on 8 April, politics professor Matthew Flinders noted the 'exasperated frustration' with which politicians and officials responded to people 'not taking seriously the advice to stay indoors', and mused:

And yet I can't help wondering if part of the problem is that the notion of crisis has simply become the new normal, particularly for millennials. Life for them must be a bit like living through a Billy Bragg song: 'Crisis after crisis, with such intensity.'

Since the millennium, they've survived against a backdrop of global financial crisis, mass refugee movement, violent revolutions in the Middle East, constant terror threats, a succession of global pandemics – SARS in 2003, bird flu in 2005, swine flu in 2009, MERS in 2012, Ebola in 2014 and now COVID in 2019. They absorb doom-laden narratives about globalization and suffer from the growth of economic precarity. They hear about the 'death' or 'end' of democracy and catastrophic climate change. Is it any wonder that mental health and well-being services are generally discussed in crisis-laden terms?[8]

Even compared to the Millennials, Generation Z have been reared on an undiluted narrative of crisis. Before Covid-19, many of the debates I engaged in about youth politics ended up focusing on the much-vaunted 'climate catastrophe', with its mantra 'we have seven years to save the planet'. In the media framing of Generation Z, Greta Thunberg has been appointed as their voice, with her shrill terror about the end of the world brought about by older generations whom the youngsters will not 'forgive'. As Chapter Five discusses, way before the economic collapse precipitated by the current crisis, the idea that these youngsters were born to shoulder the burden of low wages, crap jobs, and public debt has framed the story that others have scripted of their existence.

So it wouldn't be surprising if youngsters have become inured to crisis talk, and therefore unwilling to treat a genuine crisis with the seriousness that it deserves. Indeed, this has become a more general problem – particularly among officials and policy makers. The forecaster James Woudhuysen has drawn attention to how 'worst-case scenarios' have come to dominate thinking about a whole range of problems, particularly in the domain of health. 'This state of panic and confusion also accounts for the failure to accept the more prescient kinds of forecasts which could have helped prepare for the right healthcare strategy,' he writes.[9]

Unfortunately, however, it does not seem that a lifetime's exposure to fear makes one immune – or that the endless narrative of catastrophism makes governments reassess the wisdom of promoting fear to gain compliance with restrictions. Indeed, it seems to have had the opposite effect. A document prepared by the behavioural science sub-group SPI-B of the government's Scientific Advisory Group for Emergencies (SAGE), for discussion on 23 March (the point at which the UK's lockdown came into force), presented ramping up 'the perceived level of personal threat' as a part of an effective, evidence-based strategy for 'increasing adherence to social distancing measures'. The sub-group noted that 'there are nine broad ways of achieving behaviour change', and reviewed five of these – Education, Persuasion, Incentivisation, Coercion, and Enablement. Under 'Persuasion', the behavioural scientists argued:

> A substantial number of people still do not feel sufficiently personally threatened; it could be that they are reassured by the low death rate in their demographic group, although levels of concern may be rising...**The perceived level of personal threat needs to be increased among those who are complacent, using hard-hitting emotional messaging. To be effective this must also empower people by making clear the actions they can take to reduce the threat.**[10]

An 'evaluation grid' listed 'Use media to increase sense of

personal threat' as the second of ten 'options to rapidly increase general social distancing', and assessed its acceptability, practicability, and affordability as 'high', while the effectiveness was 'high if accompanied by other options'. The 'spill-over effects' were assessed as 'could be negative' and the 'equity' was 'uncertain' – although there is no narrative in the document about these negative aspects.

This document is striking for the coldly instrumental way in which it lays out official strategies for the emotional manipulation of the population. As a number of sociologists have noted, such strategies have been a long-running feature of the 'new public health', where the risk of danger to oneself and others is deliberately emphasized, and often inflated, to scare people away from personal behaviours deemed to be unhealthy (for example, smoking, alcohol consumption, 'junk food', and formula feeding for infants). In all these areas, negative 'spill-over' effects have been noted, with regard to the mental health impact of fear and guilt among those deemed to have chosen an 'unhealthy' course of action, and restrictions on health care support and services for people seen as less deserving of treatment because of their lifestyle choices.[11] Nonetheless, the negative effects are generally seen by policy makers as a price worth paying to encourage compliance with healthy behaviour.

Yet when extended to the realm of a population-wide public health problem, such as infectious disease, the promotion of fear has population-wide effects – which create some profound social consequences. One effect of 'using hard-hitting emotional messaging' to increase 'the perceived level of personal threat' has been to encourage inflated levels of fear among the healthy population: to the point where Robert Dingwall, Professor of Social Sciences and a member of the Government's New and Emerging Respiratory Virus Threats Advisory Group (Nervtag), was moved to caution that the strength of the message 'has effectively terrorised the population into believing that this is a disease that is going to kill you' – when 'mostly, it isn't'.[12]

Indeed, people have taken the message so much to heart that, as David Spiegelhalter, chair of the Winton Centre for Risk and Evidence Communication at Cambridge University, warned in early May, levels of fear for many ran way out of proportion to the actual personal danger they faced from Covid-19.[13] This is particularly stark in relation to young people: one poll found that nearly 60 per cent of 18-34 year olds in the UK believed that the virus was a threat to them[14] despite the fact that their risk of dying from this virus is, statistically, vanishingly small. As Spiegelhalter and Davey Smith wrote in the *British Medical Journal*:

> Covid-19 mortality closely parallels risk of death from all causes for age and sex, with age being by far the most powerful stratification variable: covid-19 mortality in people aged over 90 has been above 1.5% during the epidemic, more than 10 000 times the level seen in those under 15.[15]

Spiegelhalter has pithily summarized the age-stratified threat posed by Covid-19 in his observation that people under 50 are more likely to die suddenly because of an accident or injury than from coronavirus.[16]

There are moral questions to be asked about a campaign that deliberately sets out to terrify young people about their risk of dying from a disease that, for the most part, they are likely to experience in a mild form. Is this a responsible thing for adults to do? As Frank Furedi has argued in his discussion of the culture and politics of fear, modern societies have elevated safety to a 'first order virtue', to the point where the demand for protection from myriad threats trumps the demand for the other values historically associated with the pursuit of the good society.[17] Chapter Four discusses how our failure to distinguish between adults and children in the face of this crisis, both in terms of the age profile of the disease and the fear messaging that has been promoted to ensure compliance with the rules, speaks to a deeper tension about our ability, and willingness, to educate, socialize, and protect children.

Equally disturbing has been the way in which children and young people, as potential asymptomatic carriers of Covid-19, have been singled out as posing a particular danger to public health. What began, certainly in the UK, as a strategy designed to protect the elderly and vulnerable from the Covid-19 virus quickly morphed into a strategy focused on protecting older people from younger people, and keeping younger people apart from each other: most clearly illustrated by the prolonged closure of schools, and restrictions on socializing that applied to all age groups. Where most previous public health campaigns have promoted fear and disgust about the unhealthy body, often deploying 'shock' images of obese torsos or smokers' blackened lungs to show the consequences of unhealthy behaviour in later life, this campaign has highlighted the dangers posed by the healthy, youthful body as an unwitting vector of doom and death in the here and now. We should consider what this says about how we see young people in general, and how it might impact on how they come to see themselves.

Worrying about everything

It seems that the main effect of an endless narrative of catastrophe is not that people become impervious to fear, but increasingly open to absorbing yet more fears into their apprehension about life. This reflects deeper cultural trends, bound up with a generalized sense of powerlessness and insecurity characteristic of our modern 'risk society'.[18] At a time when people feel out of control of their destiny, heightened levels of fear around particular dangers can quickly come to dominate. This sometimes attaches to new and immediate threats, such as Covid-19. But it also attaches to the kind of risks that societies have been navigating for ages – such as allowing children to play outside with their friends unsupervised by adults, a practice that was quite normal until the 1980s, and is now regarded as fraught with danger.[19]

As Furedi has explained, in this respect the culture of the early twenty-first century has become characterized by a sense of free-floating anxiety, in which concerns about social, personal, and political problems are internalized and experienced as an ever-growing presentiment of threat. This way of processing both the threat of Covid-19, and concerns about the measures used to contain it, came through in the accounts of the young people we talked to in the early stages of the UK's lockdown. The quotes below provide a snapshot of this diffuse sense of anxiety about the virus and the impact of the measures taken to contain it.

Other people's behaviour:

I agree with the lockdown procedure but not how some people are going about it. That's dumb. The longer people congregate the longer it will last for everyone else.

Socially, this virus is dangerous because it is passed through human contact and so easily allows blame and hate to grow; there have already been numerous cases of racism and xenophobia. Moreover the implementations related to social distancing could bring about tensions in relationships – those that are separated and those that are kept together.

The effects of the disease on individuals, and on the health service:

I think the government acted well, however I think isolation lasting too long could cause more harm than good for the economy. Many of my friends are so over-worried about getting the virus themselves that even when lockdown ends they are going to continue some form of isolation. Obviously I recognize the disease is dangerous for those vulnerable, but for people my own age it is extremely unlikely to result in hospitalization so I think social distancing measures should be relaxed soon for certain members of society to reduce the impact on the economy.

With some of my family being in various stages of recovery from cancer, I have been left feeling uncertain as to what will happen to them and if a relapse occurs will they be able to receive the support they would need? This virus is not something to be forgotten about, people need to be aware of those around them who may suffer as a result of their selfishness. The pandemic is something that we need to study closely during and after in order to learn about how we can better support our society, mostly the underpaid but desperately needed frontline staff in the NHS [National Health Service].

With the NHS how is this all going to end as how are we saving something that's supposed to save us? Is it worth keeping going if it can't cope, especially as it is weakened by the pandemic?

The implications of keeping, and lifting, the lockdown:

It's inconvenient, more so for the older people, ones dying and losing their jobs, but it still makes everyone's life difficult. Bankrupting people, especially the government. I am worried about what happens when the laws get lifted, are people gonna go nuts and not wash hands next?

Looking at the projected numbers, it is obvious that governments around the world are doing the right thing by urging people to stay inside and social distance. While I think the US government was right to break everything down to the bare bones, I am most worried about what they do next. Trump has told the country differing information on what our next steps are and when we are going to 'open up' the country. My worry is that Trump moves up 'opening' the country to save the economy, when we are not fully over it.

These quotes do not show 'what young people think' about the virus or the lockdown. On this question, like every other, the Corona Generation is made up of a diverse group of individuals with different experiences and ideas. But it does confirm that teenagers are not merely potentially infectious bodies, whom we can lock indoors with Netflix and simply let out when we consider it safe to do so; they are curious minds, who are thinking about the crisis in all its dimensions. And one of the things we should be worrying about, as adults, is the degree to which we have made them do a lot of this thinking on their own.

Emma's lockdown reflections: Waking up in a dystopia

The first days after the UK's lockdown felt different. We may not have had police riding the streets, but the harsh judgement flashing almost permanently across people's faces was enough. As I walked past people on my way to the supermarket, God forbid I left the house, I was met with some slightly aggressive looks and definite attempts to walk as far away as possible. Although this was the guideline, the reaction was definitely extreme. Does the normally sane community really believe that I would be out of the house if I was a threat with symptoms? Or that the virus could spread by walking past at a normal distance? This uncanny behaviour was stifling the atmosphere in a rather dystopian way, as people were afraid to smile at passers-by.

The supermarket was yet more difficult to comprehend as stores cracked down further, limiting entry and enforcing spacing. But that's not what worried me, it was the constant flow of people's judgement and caution, they weren't just scared of the disease but of each other. And I think the young people were even more cautioned against, purely due to the prejudice about being young. Like they assumed we weren't following the rules, they didn't know where we had been. All of this due to the blown-up headlines of so-called parties across the country, which were in fact maybe five out of the millions of young people.

Fake news is a topic that has arisen with the increased use of media. As many more people are invested in the global crisis, it is now a vital time to eliminate the falsehoods to provide people with the right information. I think that it is fundamental, as in times like these people are at their most scared and will believe whatever 'authority' is telling them, and with people being scared and invested they are passionate, defending their views. This could result in a split, a polarized society, where the country is divided on their outlook, and this is dangerous.

The impact of this on Generation Z is a much higher awareness, through the increased media and reporting. We are aware of the challenges and inequalities being faced, aware that we will have to solve economic and social issues or struggle through. The inequalities highlighted give us a sense of our place and role, as we are no longer hidden from devastation. This being brought to life will have an impact on our future, to push us to try and fix the problems that previous generations couldn't.

With our generation being introduced early to local climate strikes, we have all been brought up in an 'environmentalist age', and many have become invested in this. There is a problem with global warming and plastic in the oceans, and the environment is an important issue, but I think the pandemic has helped put it into perspective in two ways: it can be changed, and it is not the ultimate sacrifice. To begin with, lockdown looked like a quick fix, as more and more people were fascinated by what looks like a cleaner environment – but they are being deceived, as this is not sustainable. It is true that there are fewer emissions and a smaller carbon footprint but that is due to the cut in production, lockdown of people in their homes, and lack of travel between countries – separating families and cancelling plans. So although environmentalists are trying to spin the wheel to blame us, it is incorrect as we can't live the next decade locked indoors with the global economy suffering. This has highlighted to many people the fragility and deeper issues with the current climate campaign, showing it needs a more sustainable reform.

Added to this, the increased focus on people's hygiene is resulting in damage as there has been a massive increase of plastic waste, especially in the amount of medical waste. The problem lies with the disposal as either it will take up a mass of landfill or will require burning, which will increase the emissions once the pandemic has subsided. However, despite the possible negative effects on the environment, I think it could be taken as a signpost showing young environmentalists a new way of thinking, as events like these show that the priorities are the population and keeping them safe: hopefully we will move to show the issues that matter most and a route to solve them, while allowing for a positive lifestyle for the majority. I think this pandemic has also shown the fragility of environmentalism especially through the lack of commitment by governments – as they are battling new problems, many environmental ones have been put on hold.

The effects of the virus could be seen as a wider wake-up call for many of Generation Z, as they are now able to properly engage and understand bigger issues in society like unemployment and rights of workers, providing a little more background for the world they live in and shifting their perspective as they come to terms with other issues. Plastic is hazardous for the environment, but necessary to save lives, and the return of its use, although consequential, shows us that despite the worries of the environmental agencies, our lives take priority, something which has not been clarified before.

Many wider problems like unemployment strike at multiple levels for us as we are at the period in our lives where we are trying to enter the labour market, which is not only complicated during the lockdown but will be for a while after, as the unemployment spikes and there is more competition. This crosses a difficulty for those still in education: as in do we go ahead with our desire for summer jobs or save the jobs for those in need? How do our needs compare to those of others? This gives us more time and less purpose, and with a lack of opportunity to make a difference we are stuck in a period of unspecified time, as there are so many restrictions on trying to prevent the spread there are limited opportunities for under-18s to volunteer and help.

Issues with the stability of the family can arise, as there are some households which are more prone to being unsafe and without access to school the students have no support to help them in times of crisis, with further complications and dangers as the emergency services are restricted or preoccupied. The depression and financial difficulties caused by the instability in the economy could heavily affect the income of these families and therefore push them into deeper holes. Along with the lack of school this means that these homes have no distraction from themselves and makes it difficult for children to focus on their education, disadvantaging them further. This highlights the depth of economic inequality, as although many people will be hit by the recession it is these young people who will suffer the most. Although some may get to regain the education, it shows the deeper effects the coronavirus will have on many people's lives and why this will not be over shortly; it will require institutions and individuals to regain focus and discipline to keep lives on track.

As to the generational divide, I believe there is less of a

divide between ourselves and our grandparents than to those our parents' age or younger. As we go to our grandparents for comfort they let us innocently get through, but with those older than us, being our future co-workers, we see more of a divide as we are getting tired of labels, of snowflake, reckless, useless, when many of us are the opposite – sticking closely to rules and guidelines, we are in fact a generation of goody two-shoes. But this is also a generalization.

Chapter 3

Virtual intimacies

Since the invention of television, commentators have loved to overstate and decry the detrimental impact of technology on children's physical and mental health. Time and again, we have been warned that violent films and video games desensitize young people, leading to 'real-life' violence; that the easy availability of pornography promotes a robotic misogyny among adolescent boys; that the 'always on' nature of social media platforms facilitates bullying and FOMO (fear of missing out) anxiety. Empirical studies of the evidence behind these presumptions tend to be much more equivocal: digital interactions are mediated through human relationships, with parents, peers, and teachers; and many of these actually become the bridge through which children can interact with each other (for example, multi-player gaming).

But we don't have to get all technophobic to acknowledge that different technologies mediate culture and relationships in different ways, and that some things are lost while others are gained. The kind of immersion encouraged by reading a book is different to that demanded from watching a film; the encounter with a weekly TV series aired at a fixed time on the family set is different from binge-watching Netflix in a bedroom; pornography is different to sex, and readily-available digitized porn invites a different response than furtive encounters with somebody's illicit stash of *Playboy* magazines. And of course, to follow through my friend's musing on the 'fascinating social experiment' we are currently conducting, we have never studied the effects on a mass of children and young people who are not only logged in to every new platform going, but also deprived of 'real' everyday interactions with anyone except their parents and siblings. (In 'normal' times, such an experiment would be considered unethical.)

It would be wrong to second-guess the results; to rush to a conclusion that it has been harmful or fine. But when considering how this crisis might impact on generational consciousness, we don't have to declare whether the 'media effect' will be positive, negative, or benign – we only need to acknowledge that there will be an effect. The sudden shift in norms and expectations framing the way that young people have been forced to consider their personal, social interactions has not happened on this scale, or with this intensity, since the Second World War. Those coming of age right now have a heightened sense of how things were before lockdown compared to the period during and after lockdown, which will give them an experience of growing up that is distinct from anybody older or younger.

But what is really different about the period of lockdown is the extent to which these technologies have become young people's sole source of interaction with the outside world: their friends, teachers, extended family, and the news. This prolonged period of isolation from physical contact is likely to have a significant impact on young people's growing-up – particularly for those on the cusp of independence, who keenly experience the difference between life before and after social distancing.

Social media in isolation

Leah, 17, and Laura, 15, are sisters living in London. Both wrote about how much they had valued social media during the period of lockdown, for allowing them to 'speak to my friends and family whenever I want, even if it is not in person', keep the amount of contact 'as close to normal as possible'. But they also talked wistfully about the downsides, and expressed a yearning for what they called 'real social interaction'. 'While it is a good way to communicate, it is easy to spend hours on social media without doing much,' wrote Laura. 'So, I am trying to balance staying in contact with my friends while still getting things done.' She continued:

> Although I am glad that I have the ability to be able to communicate with my friends through social media and I am trying to make the most out of this, I also know that it is not the same as and cannot make up for the lack of real social interaction which is one of the things that I am missing most at the moment.

For Leah, one of the main issues facing her and her friends during lockdown was how to keep their conversations over social media 'real'. She explained:

> There is only a certain amount of conversation that you can have with someone without going out and experiencing real life interaction – this applies to friendship and also in regards to dating as we are stuck in a period of time where the only way of keeping these relationships going is having conversations over social media or FaceTime which is really difficult to maintain or to keep feeling substantial over a long period of time.

When thinking about how the Covid-19 crisis might frame the Corona Generation's sense of itself, the tension between physical and digital interaction poses some important questions. This generation has grown up taking social media for granted – unlike some older people, it has not had to train itself to accept stilted, pixelated chats as an alternative to 'real' or 'normal' interaction. 'Our generation aren't strangers to communicating through social media, so as time has gone on it has become easier,' observed Ruby, 17. She suggested that the experience was even 'good preparation' for going off to university, when 'in some ways this sort of communication, through social media and over the phone, is what I will have to rely upon when keeping in contact with old friends / my boyfriend / family'.

But at the same time, it was striking how often the phrases 'real' and 'normal' recurred in their accounts, as a counter-position to the experience of communicating *only* via social media. There was a wistful sense of loss, and a yearning to get back to physical encounters. These were not only encounters with intimate others – in many ways, established personal relationships, with grandparents, sexual partners, or best friends were seen as relatively straightforward to navigate online; and despite the sense that things were 'not the same', there was also a hope that it could improve the quality of these encounters. 'My family lives far away but yet I feel that I am closer to them as ever as we speak more,' said Zoe, 18, adding that, 'Things like this bring people together.'

Amy, 15, wrote:

We haven't completely lost intimacy, however it does feel distant at the moment. It's harder but it's manageable. It's given us time to learn more about each other because we've been having regular conversations. Although there's going to be difficulties not seeing each other, we're mature enough to work around that. And it's going to be so special when we finally get to see each other again in person.

What struck them more deeply, though, was the absence of casual interactions – from being stuck in school with a peer group not of your choosing, to being out and about in the community. For some, there was a sense of being freed from the constraints of friendship groups, and having permission to hang out only with, as Laura put it, your 'true friends':

At school there is the constant pressure to spend every day

with each other and on top of that, people often get judged based on who they're associating themselves with. Now, there is no obligation to spend time with classmates and there is no in-school reputation to worry about. As a result, the people we frequently talk to on social media are the people who we genuinely want to talk to. This has shown me who my true friends are as if we can maintain our friendship through these uncertain times, we should be able to get through anything.

While close friendships and relationships with intimate partners via social media were generally considered to be manageable, and were maybe even deepened by the experience of lockdown, these posed some challenges. For example, Ruby talked about how her relationship with her boyfriend changed 'from seeing each other all the time to it becoming almost like a long-distance relationship, which we were not fully prepared for'.

But for the young people we spoke to, the bigger problem was the wider social interaction, which had previously been contextualized through school, and through the wider peer dynamics that the experience of school creates. As Emma writes below, having these taken-for-granted relationships suddenly stripped away plunges young people into a position where they have to make a deliberate decision about who, and when, to hang out with online, and what they are going to do or talk about. Poppy, 16, said that lockdown has had 'different effects on different relationships', bringing uncertainty regarding relationships with 'people at school who you would meet up with or talk to, but don't message outside of school'. Bettie, 16, said: 'It is so strange because I would see people frequently, and despite new connections, I feel detached.'

Mark, a 21-year-old student in Pittsburgh, wrote:

This whole situation has made me realize how much of a social person I am. I love all the different interactions I had with people all over the place. I miss the little banter I had with the workers at the Einstein's Bagels where I would get breakfast. I miss the conversations I had with the older security guard at the building where I practice. These little interactions would get me through my day.

The pressure imposed by the absence of 'little interactions' may not sound like such a big deal, but it is a lot to ask of teenagers and young adults, for whom relationships are frequently changeable and dramatic, and develop within an external context that is framed and led by adults, albeit at arm's length – the structure of the school day, the restrictions on who can have a party, where they are allowed to go, what time they have to be home by. Chapter Four discusses how the family isolation demanded by lockdown has thrown this relationship between the adult and child worlds into disarray. The adults are more obviously there, in the form of a parent who is ever-present, but their authority to permit or restrict activities outside the family is curtailed by the demand for everybody to follow the same law.

There was a sense of social worlds shrinking, as reliance on communication with those closest to you right now truncated the possibilities of developing relationships in the future. For those 15-, 16-, and 17-year-olds who were planning to return to school in the autumn, their frustrations were generally focused around the loss of the experiences they were expected to be having now – the intense rite of passage provided by exam season, followed by its euphoric rewards: the prom, the long summer holidays hanging out with friends, the transition to the next phase of studying. The cost of these interruptions is high, not least in the dismissive message that has been sent to young people about the importance of their education. But for the older ones, on the cusp of stepping away from their families and to university or the world of work, there was a larger sense of being hobbled on the path to adulthood. Leah wrote:

I feel that this is particularly significant for me and my friends as we are at the age where we are becoming adults (it is most likely that I will be turning 18 in lockdown) and therefore, this is the time in which we should be becoming independent. We had been planning this summer for a long time as it would be our first real opportunity to have complete freedom and independence. Because of this, most of our time is being spent planning and thinking about how we will make the most of this freedom once this is over, but this is causing us to wish this whole period of time away as we are only really using it to think about the future which feels like a real shame.

Being caught in a situation where it is possible only to 'think about the future', rather than ground those thoughts in the lived experience of the present, is potentially destabilizing – particularly in a context where the future is framed as uncertain, frightening, and likely to be grim. Gracie, 21, suggested that the pandemic has already had a 'massive impact' on those who have completed their education, 'on their futures and their sense of self, as they are feeling a great sense of loss for so many things, they feel as if a crucial and exciting time has been taken away from them'. She continued:

The effects may not last decades but will massively shape the next five years. Many are forced to move back and become fully reliant on their parents in a time where they were just planning to move forward, to become fully independent with jobs and internships already lined up (many of which have been cancelled or postponed). It also creates great uncertainty for so many as they are stepping into the workplace for the first time when it is at its weakest and jobs are on the line and unstable, in a time when they need experience and guidance but there is none to give.

The sense of loss that Gracie describes is partly due to the wrenching away of 'many of the exciting traditions and milestones' that have marked the path to adulthood. But it also speaks to the rocking of a more grounded approach to the future, the more immediate loss of the attachments formed at this point in their lives – what they mean right now, and where they could lead to. She continued:

> I have FaceTimed my closest friends but the relationships I valued that weren't so close, which were on the fringes, suffered as I didn't get to say goodbye to anyone or to further the relationship. And who's to say what that relationship could have been, and I think it could have been more which is really painful. There was someone who mentioned their parents met during the senior spring so to all of us it was like what if we missed the love of our lives. But more the overall feeling that we missed something so big. The relationships you have with your friends, I used to go driving with my best friend to a nearby restaurant and play music really loud, and I would sit there and think this is the moment that I really value, which is stupid because it is so little, not like a ball or graduation but that's what I'm missing. A fifteen-minute drive that I don't usually get.

Media dependency

Every new app or platform has generated a new set of potential dangers, either to do with the dangerous strangers lurking on the web (paedophiles, scammers, promoters of self-harm), or the way these technologies facilitate harmful encounters within 'real-life' peer groups (bullying, sexting, pranking, and so on). Parents have been variously warned, trained, and terrified about the myriad hazards of social media, on the grounds that our 'digital native' children will be several steps ahead of us in accessing all this bad stuff – so we have to engage in a campaign of constant, yet futile, vigilance.

Now, parents across the Western world will be feeling a deep sense of irony that the lockdown encouraged children and teenagers to do the very thing that they have been warned against for years: get intimate with their screens, and conduct their social lives via apps. All that moaning about how the decline in outdoor play is having a terrible effect on children's physical and mental health, and how the open space of the internet makes children's encounters difficult to contain or control, suddenly got very quiet. Into the silence came a load of pragmatic justifications about why, thanks to their love of social media, the so-called 'i-Gen' wouldn't suffer too much from lockdown. After all, they spent their days gaming or streaking or WhatsApp-ing or whatever-ing anyway – what difference would it make?

It is this gap in understanding – the inability to form an empathetic understanding of young people's interactions online – that lies at the heart of the much-lamented 'digital divide' between adults and kids. In the moment, there is little that adults can, or should, do to shape this experience – the personal journey towards growing up is always a lonely one, which can only be shared by those going through it at the same age, in the same place, at the same time. Hence the anguished cry of teenagers over the decades: 'You don't understand!'

But where adult society can, and should, be taking more responsibility for our teenagers' experiences is in the way it mediates the social crisis that we are experiencing. In this regard, we should be paying much more attention to their encounters with the news.

Watching the UK government's Coronavirus briefing one evening, with the dutiful announcement of the number of new hospital admissions, my daughter Annia, aged 13, said, 'I can't tell if that's good or bad.' I had no answer to that. When her phone alerted her to the death of a 13-year-old boy, she was distraught; one morning, the first thing she said to me was, 'Mum, it's bad news, we've had more than 10,000 deaths.' Trying to contextualize this undoubtedly bad news through a discussion of the difficulty of differentiating between those who died 'with' or 'of' Covid-19[1]; the international disparities in testing; and the relatively low risk posed to young people's health by the disease seems cold and weirdly inappropriate. The only permitted response seems to be to agree how terrible it is, and to affirm the message that we should stay at home.

Yet contextualizing the crisis is exactly the discussion we should be having with young people. In all other circumstances, parents and educators are issued with warnings about the dangers posed to impressionable young minds by the echo chambers and rumour mills of social media, the proliferation of 'fake news', media bias, and the irresponsible use of statistics. In the frenzied media coverage of Covid-19, we have seen all these problems writ large – to the point that it is genuinely difficult even for adults with some understanding of science and mathematics to work out what precisely is going on.

For example: when different countries are using different tests for Covid-19, testing different parts of their populations, and using different rules for reporting Covid-19 deaths, it is clearly very difficult to gain an accurate picture of the incidence and spread of the virus at a national level, let alone to make international comparisons. But day by day, hour by hour, we have been bombarded by another grim update to the ghoulish league table of which country is 'the worst' – measured by numbers ('UK COVID-19 hospital death toll passes 10,000 mark'; 'US death toll passes 2,000 in a single day')[2] in the absence of contextual data such as the size and age structure of the populations concerned, or the co-morbidities and other factors involved in a proportion of these deaths.

The balance between informing ourselves about the pandemic and losing ourselves in the drama of the death toll is a delicate one – particularly when it comes to the discussions we have with young people. However, it is complicated by a widespread lack of agreement on what is the news, and which news we should trust. Young people's drift away from established news channels to more segmented social media has been a discussion point for some years. This is not limited to kids – it is a wider trend, associated with the rise of internet platforms, the growth of 'citizen journalism' and the blogosphere, and the increasing polarization of political views and cultural preferences. Concerns about the rationale for, or the decline of, public service broadcasting are heightened by low levels of trust in the state and the media.

But while some of us at least remember a time when we gathered our knowledge of world events from 'a newspaper', or when families would watch or listen to a particular news broadcast, the Corona Generation has grown up with rolling news accessible at any time, from a whole range of sources. In 'normal', non-coronavirus times, this could make it difficult even to answer the question, 'what's in the news?' with any consistency. I realized this a few years ago, when setting my students the task of looking at the newspapers and picking a topical social policy issue that was being discussed that week: 'the newspapers' were clearly alien, and there seemed to be no particular online source that was used. My kids gain their news variously through Snapchat or Instagram, and from 'breaking news' alerts from a range of sources.

So even when it is clear that 'the news' is the Covid-19 crisis, and that we are all probably ingesting too much of it for our own good, we are not necessarily sharing the same news. We don't much trust the news that we do watch; although the pandemic has been delivering 'record audiences' for news programmes, polls suggest ambivalence about how far people trust the media to give a balanced account.[3] Meanwhile, suspicion of 'fake news' coexists with a sharp cultural polarization between those who rely on particular news channels or publications for their understanding of 'the truth'. News outlets increasingly play the role of activist campaigners, competing to be first with the shocking statistics and lurid headlines, and demanding that the government responds to the latest claim or proposal. As public cynicism about the news has grown, even the pretence of objectivity has been downgraded in favour of clickbait.

That we are gripped by the media coverage is understandable, of course. We want to know more about this disease, which threatens to ravage our loved ones and has become the basis on which 'normal life' has been indefinitely suspended. As democratic societies, we *need* to know about the trajectory of the disease in order to judge whether the measures taken to suppress it are currently justified; never has a free press been more important, in reporting the facts as they are known (however partial), and in providing a platform for disagreements among epidemiologists, scientists, and a whole range of other voices debating what we know and what we should do about it.

But there is also a danger that, as the criminologist Simon Cottee puts it, we are indulging an unhealthy obsession with 'pandemic porn'[4], which does not increase our understanding of the disease, so much as it threatens to dehumanize and desensitize us. Confined to our houses, our only understanding can come from watching the numbers unfold on the TV and internet; and we have no daily contact with others to keep our fears and prejudices in check. Young people are witnessing an historical moment – but as passive observers of it, rather than active participants in it. By cutting them adrift from the taken-for-granted interactions with friends or other adults that can absorb and contextualize these fears, we seem to be taking our responsibilities to children extraordinarily lightly.

Emma's lockdown reflections: The gap where casual interactions used to be

Growing up we increasingly saw schools trying to limit our use of social media, warning us of the dangers of living our lives online. But with the lockdown shutting out all other entrances for the outside world it is all that remains of our personal lives, promoted by governments and schools as the saviour of the Covid crisis. I don't deny that the technology has greatly aided my sanity in the lockdown but the interactions are not the same, as even when using FaceTime or Houseparty you feel distant, the encounters are more strained as you are forced into a conversation when in reality there is little to be said – everyone is living in a monotonous parallel. This shift in conversation and interaction is upsetting for Generation Z, but at least we are conscious of what we are missing and itching to get back. Those much younger than us are in a dangerous place, as in their pivotal period of social development they are trapped online.

The most dangerous effects of isolated social media use are its normalization over physical interaction, and the narrowed and much more selective interaction. Before, you wouldn't expect people to be on their phone while they were having a conversation or out with a friend, but what scares me about the change of social media use is that this will no longer be seen as abnormal. With social media currently being the only way to communicate with others, not just your close family, it provides a constant distraction due to your desire to remain active as your wider self; understandably you prioritize your messages over the repetitive conversations with your family, but I think this could be damaging as it becomes more frequent. The line of normality has been moved but where has it been moved to?

The use of social media is also dangerous in allowing for

much more selective communication, where people are choosing fewer people to talk to, and messaging someone is seen as much more direct and therefore more daunting. This is damaging to the weaker relationships that are vital to people's daily lives, with those you don't directly rely on but encounter and converse with frequently, who keep memories alive and things moving on. Apps like Houseparty allow for closed rooms, a very new experience, where you can publicly see people online with others but cannot join. The more frequent the use of these communications, the more direct media will become, leading to stronger core relationships but much weaker outer ones causing fragile bonds and isolation or insecurity. This is devastating for those who are more naturally insecure or less confident, as it is much more frightening approaching into an online conversation than casually joining due to an eye signal across a room, making social interaction much harder to navigate.

The lack of casual interaction seems to be what is hitting people the most, and it seems to have highlighted that not all interaction can be replaced or be taken in the form of a phone screen. There are multiple connections and interactions missing; conversation that may not be deep and meaningful but keep the day moving, the man in the corner shop in the morning, the girl in the form room you would never think to message. This seems to be the biggest loss for me, as the school shut and at a time of solidarity (pulling each other through the exams); my expanded relationships have been drastically cut, along with the prevalence of casual gossip – there is no longer anything else to talk about, making the world a much more serious place.

At an age where we are moving through the importance of different types of conversation I feel stripped of the last pieces of innocence that I was holding onto, the innocence attached to meaningless conversations, joking with the boys or making fun of teenage relationships – this has evaporated leaving a hole filled with pandemic politics and rational conversation. I suppose this is eye-opening to some, but to many others it is simply boring, as they are not ready to completely join adult conversation but are stripped of much else to discuss.

Furthermore, the complexity and informality of most relationships has really been shown, as the use of media is not only the norm but the only method of communication, meaning that you are limited to those closest to you. Many of us hadn't realized the pressure of messaging a distant friend or an acquaintance; it seems like a much bigger deal than we remembered, as you try to push conversation it seems to be more unnatural and fractured, you're not sure what to say as the monotonous 'how are you?' has a fairly communal answer and most relationships are not close enough to discuss deeper feelings and memories. This, added to the mass of apps like Skype, Zoom, or Houseparty, makes you very aware of clichés and groups; it is hard if you are swimming in the middle, as you can see who is available and online. You question whether the relationship is enough to reach into or alternatively they may think that it was odd and you should leave them to it, making a simple 'hey, how are you?' seem a lot bigger than usual.

However, I think it is starting to show the importance and strength of many more distant relationships, and I think this will increase. With people fighting through isolation and boredom there is a sense of recognition that this is temporary and a sense of solidarity, where we know we will see each other in the late summer (fingers crossed), and that although we may not speak in the closer months that we will be back to normal by then, a sense strengthened by anticipation and excitement for when this is all over. The sense of space, although tedious, is giving people the needed capacity to breathe and reminding us of what our physical relationships are worth.

The relationships with extended family have also changed greatly over the years, as there is a sub-communication going on through social media. Although many people may not think about their extended kin at a time like this, to me it has brought to light the strange weakness of these relations. I think that the development of social media has weakened many of these bonds further, as not only do people now live further away but they are more separate, and there is less need to call or privately message as their updates are available on Facebook; therefore the only conversation to be had is through a birthday card or a fleeting moment at a family event.

The coronavirus has highlighted these relations to me as although there is not an abundance of family events around, they are a definite feature, and their being banned strikes the question of who these people are. There is a weakness in bonds between people who live miles away, maybe seeing each other once every 2 years. For those who are younger and not yet in touch on Facebook there is often very little contact with elders leading me to wonder what it will be like in the future. Will we lose contact as we move further away, engulfed by developments in the world and those directly around you, or will the ease of online communications strengthen the bonds with your more extended family?

The cancellation or diminishing of funerals has also had a massive impact on the value we place on our interactions, especially in the family, as although for many reasons the temporary change to funerals may be seen as the necessary and only rational option due to the travelling and social distancing, it seems to disregard the basis of solidarity in families and communities as you're limiting the celebration of someone's life to those very closest to them and forcing everyone else to grieve behind closed doors. How does this affect the overall sense of community and extended support? The government is not only suggesting but enforcing a state of self-sufficiency where there is only virtual and forced support from a limited range of people, further degrading the importance of relationships with a much broader range of people and types. It reminds us of the importance and value in our family, as we are now stopped from seeing them when we need them most.

Identity is often seen to be a huge part of Generation Z, with the focus on LGBTQ+ and gender politics, and with all of this seen to some extent in schools it often makes it more difficult for those without a distinct label. However, it can also be said that there is an element of this sense of identity in everything, it isn't just your gender but your views on environmental change, politics, and now even lockdown. People group in terms of their identity, so being away from constant judgement and boxing is refreshing. Lockdown is giving us space from society and its pressures, but more importantly separating society from ourselves as we are more outwardly invested in the wider problems we are facing.

As we grow up we are constantly struggling with the changing dynamics of ourselves, but now being trapped (for many of us) with the stable personalities of our parents does give us space to breathe and refigure what we want to do with our lives and who we want to be. As clichéd as it sounds, we enter this time when we are most distracted by each other, our futures and exams, so with all of that put on hold it gives us space to breathe and think. This is a luxury we don't usually have, but could be newly recognized as beneficial; as there is a more diverse world, we need time away from pressures to figure out the path ahead.

Therefore, there is a positive being seen in the lives of young people, as there is less pressure on our sense of self, less pressure to perform, label, and show yourself to the world – we no longer need to be restricted. People are more comfortable and relaxed in themselves as the focus is no longer on them, even those not invested in the outcomes and politics of the situation recognize there is something big going on. A more relaxed attitude to life has been widely welcomed and accepted at a time where everyone was trying to appear their best and most stable. I think it is important to recognize that for a lot of people, although Covid-19 has brought more fear, uncertainty, and anxiety, it has taken a lot of smaller identity issues away.

Chapter 4

The adult world retreats

'We are not, repeat not, closing schools now,' insisted UK Prime Minister Boris Johnson on 12 March, arguing that the scientific advice was that school closures would do 'more harm than good at this stage'.[1] By the end of the following week, the nation's bewildered children had been kicked out of their classrooms for what many believed would be an extended Easter break – a holiday that would last for 4 weeks, rather than the usual 2. Yet over 2 months later, the vast majority of children were still at home – with no clear idea of when, or how, they would be going back.

On 7 May, the World Bank reported that due to Covid-19, schools were closed for 85 per cent of children worldwide.[2] *Eighty-five per cent.*

Even as some countries began tentative measures to ease lockdown, many children were consigned to stay-home policies until the autumn. In the UK, proposals for a limited opening of schools on 1 June to children in some year groups became a full-fledged political battle, with teaching unions demanding 'clear, scientific published evidence' showing that this would be safe for staff, and many parents reporting that they would be too scared to send their kids back.[3]

As I write, it is doubtful whether schools will return to normal even by September 2020. In a hard-hitting article headlined 'Many Wealthy Parents Won't Send Kids Back to School This Fall; That's a Disaster Waiting to Happen', Kiera Butler, senior editor of *Mother Jones* magazine, picked up on some tweeting anxiety among middle-class American parents. 'No way we go back to a regular classroom without a vaccine,' wrote one. 'We'll be sending our kid to an online school. Not ideal but there's too much of a risk otherwise, particularly in a deep red area where people aren't adhering to most of the distancing guidelines,' said another.[4] Universities, meanwhile, are being tasked with developing 'contingency plans' to run courses online in the event that campuses remain closed in the autumn, or are forced to close by another lockdown. By May 2020, some had already announced that they intended to teach mainly online for the 2020-21 academic year.

How did we get to this place? As discussed in Chapter Two, Covid-19 does not pose a great threat to the majority of children and young people. The big fear, which prompted the initial closure of schools, is that kids might be viral 'super spreaders', as they seem to be with flu; yet as the weeks have passed more evidence has challenged this assumption, with some studies suggesting they are less likely to transmit it than adults.[5] Given the morbidity and mortality profile of Covid-19, it is understandable that some individual teachers will have good cause for concern about working in a crowded school while the virus is still spreading, and they should be protected. But as a group, the age and ethnicity profile of the teaching profession in the UK puts them at relatively low risk: around three-quarters are women, almost 90 per cent are white, and their average age is around 39.[6]

The trepidation with which the world regards opening up schools is down to two things. First, it speaks to the overwhelming impact of fear, where the imperative of safety trumps all other values, including freedom and, in this case, education. With Covid-19, the focus on safety from this infection has even trumped other physical and mental health dangers resulting from prolonged school closures. As Lee Hudson, consultant paediatrician and chief of mental health at Great Ormond Street Hospital, wrote in *The Guardian*:

I find myself coming back to the same question. Are we

thinking about this the wrong way round – is it not more risky instead to keep our children at home?[7]

Second, it speaks to the shallowness of the value attached to education. This is ironic given the rhetorical importance politicians and policymakers attach to it. Former British Prime Minister Tony Blair famously described his 'three main priorities' for the New Labour government (1997-2010) as 'Education, Education, Education'.[8] To this end, early years education was expanded, education to 18 made compulsory, and 50 per cent of young people expected to go on to university. The subsequent Coalition and Conservative governments continued to emphasize the importance of education, with reforms to GCSE and A-level exams to make them more rigorous, and a ramping up of the compulsion to attend, fining parents for taking their kids out of school on holiday.

Yet when confronted with a crisis in which a series of tough decisions need to be made, education suddenly dropped down the priority list. Technology has allowed schools to set and mark work and communicate with children, and with dedicated and flexible teaching, we can hope that many kids will be able to catch up on the curriculum. But the symbolic significance of the retreat from schooling – which for years has been presented to young people as the most important days of their lives, if not the best – should not be underestimated.

Suspended in animation

The teenagers we talked to described the confusion that characterized the weeks leading up to the closure of schools. At the time, this was as exciting as it was unnerving. Some experienced the turmoil as a welcome break from the predictable treadmill of normal school, allowing them time to relax and pursue their hobbies and interests, and the cancellation of the dreaded summer exams as a big relief. 'I was initially very, overly excited,' said Becca, 16. 'It was the coolest thing ever. I was out with two of my friends and they were both ecstatic.' But it quickly sank in that this was a really big deal: 'I called loads of others and no one else was excited. Lots of girls were upset, and realized it was bigger and more drastic.'

Even those disappointed by the cancellation of exams believed that it was the right decision in the circumstances. Indeed, given the febrile uncertainty that prevailed in the UK before the virus peaked, it is hard to see how a different decision could have been made: as Becca put it, 'In this situation it wasn't fair to expect teenagers to revise as the world fell apart.' But as the weeks went on, it was not just the world outside of school that seemed to be falling apart, but their own plans for the future.

This was expressed particularly by A-level students who planned to go to university. Zoe, 18, described a sense of 'pressure, anxiety and sadness as we thought we would get to the university we wanted to be at through exams and providing the results. Many try not to worry but there is an underlying sense of unease as we are not sure of the future and acceptance by universities.' Ruby described the cancellation of her A-levels, 'something it has felt as if my entire school life has been building up to', as 'surreal':

It takes away from us a sense of finality and accomplishment, and a period of intense study that would have meant we were more prepared for the greater amount of work that will be demanded from us at university.

'Personally, the greatest effect has been less about my grades and more about my transition between schools, socially and academically: the last few months with my friends and teachers were cut short, and there are now more uncertainties about moving to a new school,' said Nancy, 16.

'Having university open days cancelled has led to some

anxiety about my future, how am I supposed to know where to apply if I can't actually see my potential place of study?' said Cleo, 17.

The sudden removal of the rites of passage associated with academic performance, such as exam results day and university open days, would have been experienced more starkly by the young people we talked to – mainly high-achieving middle-class girls, who were invested in this route – than by the teenage cohort in general. But paradoxically, it is because these are the rites associated with success and privilege that taking them away is more significant for *all* young people.

Rightly or wrongly, today's youth has been raised in a culture that prizes school performance above just about any other achievement or personal quality, and constantly emphasizes the rewards that accrue from higher levels of qualification. Although many are critical of this one-sided approach to 'success', pointing out that doing well in exams does not always lead to better jobs or greater personal fulfilment, it sets the bar for social expectations about young people's chances in general. Essentially, a 'deficit model' operates, which assumes that those who don't succeed in education are less likely to succeed in life.

In different times, the sudden retreat from an obsession with exams and grades could be seen as a useful corrective to the one-sided focus on academic success. Unfortunately, as the next chapter discusses, the employment prospects for the 'Corona Generation' are already being framed as dire – and the generation cast out from school has also been symbolically blocked from engaging in other aspects of social and economic life. The disenchantment experienced by those who were on the established path to success may well fuel cynicism in younger cohorts about why they should even bother. As Georgina, aged 11, remarked:

I think it is pretty disgusting they cancelled exams, as even

I think and worry a lot about them now, and your whole secondary life is based and dedicated to them so for adults to turn around in two weeks and effectively cancel your life is pretty bad.

As for those who were already struggling in education, the suspension of education has meant that the onus falls on them to keep on struggling, but on their own.

Remote teachers

For those young people who were not in exam years, the experience of having to keep up with their studies at home raised other issues. However diligent schools were being in setting work and communicating with students, they felt that they were having to work things out alone. 'As a year 12 student coronavirus has led to some disruption in my school life, from having to teach myself three A-levels including a foreign language at home to having had an A-level exam affected by the virus,' wrote Cleo. 'Teaching myself has been difficult during this time mostly because I do not know this content, particularly with my language course I am essentially teaching myself to be fluent which is near impossible without anyone to correct my mistakes.'

Laura described the 'transition to online schooling' as 'the biggest adjustment that I have had to make during this lockdown'. She recognized that she was fortunate to go to a school that was 'providing lessons of sorts, with a certain level of structure'. However:

Despite the online schooling provided, I am relying heavily on myself to make sure that I am still on track. It is difficult to know if I am teaching myself the right content, which is resulting in me spending more time on each subject than I normally would do at school. It also means that when we do go back to school, a lot of content will be rushed to ensure we can get through our courses on time, once again making the student responsible for a lot of their education. While it is good to become independent learners, these are not the ideal circumstances, as not only are GCSEs stressful enough but lots of the content cannot be taught from home.

Some highly-motivated, academically-able, or just plain bored students might well prefer a pattern of study that allows them to work at their own pace, and find it easy enough to learn sufficient curriculum content to pass their exams. But for others, it will be a different story.

Even in 'normal' times, kids from better-off backgrounds do better in school because their families can top up the resources offered by state education. During lockdown, huge gaps have opened up between private schools, who are desperately trying to justify their fees with state-of-the art Zoom lessons and personalized support. The online provision offered within state schools varies widely[9] – as does pupils' ability to engage with what the schools are offering. Children who were already demotivated or struggling, who don't have a computer, good WiFi connection, or space in which they can do their work, and whose families lack the funds to buy additional resources or tutors to help their kids catch up, are likely to fall further behind once we have evacuated them from education for 5 months.

In the USA, where the gap between educational 'haves' and 'have nots' is even wider than in the UK, the consequence of school closures combined with ongoing parental fears is likely to have even starker social consequences. Butler's article in *Mother Jones* predicts some 'serious downstream consequences' of the middle-class flight from public schools. Noting that it is already clear that Black and Hispanic communities are 'bearing the brunt of the disease', she warns that, 'White middle and upper middle-class parents may avoid sending their kids to schools with large Black and Hispanic populations, because they will begin to associate the virus with those communities — and by doing so, they could actually make those stereotypes more true.' Many of the parents in these communities, such as those who work in retail, package and food delivery, and in hospitals, 'don't have the option to hide out from the virus at home'.

One casualty of the divide, Butler suggests, is that 'the COVID-19 crisis could undo efforts to integrate schools – which is bad news for all students'. Promoting some kind of educational equality across the social divisions of class and race was a hard enough endeavour even before Covid-19, and the educational polarities in the UK and USA were already stubbornly entrenched. Yet the decades of painstaking progress here could be unravelled in the blink of an eye, in a context where families are suffering the economic effects of Covid-19 in a more polarized way.

Even for the most fortunate of children, the experience of being catapulted into a premature state of 'independent learning' will be a jolt. By evacuating children from the classroom and cutting them off from each other, adult society suspended its responsibility to the education and socialization of the young. School isn't always pleasant for children, and it's certainly not always fun. But it plays a crucial role in socializing children, and providing their lives with structure and meaning. School provides a context for young people to form and navigate new relationships, and gradually develop their sense of self and independence. Lessons provide the core of school, but not the total experience – the conversations with friends, the interactions with teachers, the classroom dynamics that provide children with a sense of being part of something.

During lockdown, children have been cut adrift from the norms and expectations that have framed their lives from the age of four, and have been cut off from each other. The hurried, valiant efforts that schools have made to keep the individualized, online study going might provide children with a necessary focus and distraction from the chaos that surrounds them, but it's hardly education in any meaningful sense.

Ultimately, education is a moral project. It is about showing our responsibility, as adults, to the next generation – helping them to understand the world and their place in it, and the importance of education in leading them through. Writing in the 1950s, the political philosopher Hannah Arendt argued:

> Education is the point at which we decide whether we love the world enough to assume responsibility for it and by the same token save it from that ruin which, except for renewal, except for the coming of the new and young, would be inevitable. And education, too, is where we decide whether we love our children enough not to expel them from our world and leave them to their own devices, nor to strike from their hands their chance of undertaking something new, something unforeseen by us, but to prepare them in advance for the task of renewing a common world.[10]

This is particularly important in times of crisis. Yet schools have been stripped of their ability, and responsibility, to help look after young people, and guide them through this disturbing and frightening time. In slamming the school gates shut, adult society expelled young people from the public world – and compromised their private lives as well.

Blurred boundaries

The relationship between school and home has never been easy. Children and parents alike chafe at the routine, the rules, and the petty injustices of the demands of school, while teachers' struggles to engage recalcitrant pupils are often made harder by antagonistic mums and dads. In recent years, these tensions have come more starkly to the fore, as policy has blurred the boundaries between the responsibilities of home and school.

In her discussion of the rise of an increasingly interventionist agenda in family policy since the 1990s, the sociologist Val Gillies writes:

> Perhaps, the clearest example of this transformation in the construction of state / family relations concerns the semi-permeable boundaries that are now expected to be maintained between family homes and schools. The once separate domains of the teacher and parent have become far less distinct.[11]

Gillies notes that '[p]arental involvement in a child's education is presented as an essential practice, alongside an expectation that opportunities for educational development in the home will consistently be provided'. One example of this is the formalization of 'Home School Agreements', which 'can specify the exact nature of these requirements, detailing the number of hours parents are expected to read to children and the written feedback that must be passed to the teacher'.

While parents have been tasked with teaching, writes Gillies, schools have become charged with responsibility for many things usually associated with parenting. Examples of this include the expectation that teachers will 'commonly address emotional and social aspects of pupils' lives without recourse to parents', and the 2003 'Every Child Matters' framework, which extended the remit of schools to the safeguarding and general welfare of their pupils:

> Within this wide reaching policy initiative, teachers are positioned as playing a key role in the early identification of children at risk of harm and are expected to involve themselves in securing the safety and appropriate

development of their pupils. This responsibility has been acted out in a variety of ways, including for example lunch box inspections to confiscate unhealthy foods packed by parents, and school intervention in pupil misdemeanours taking place at weekends.

In the fraught discussion about school closures, the problems caused by removing the welfare function of schools were widely anticipated. Footage from US states of the army handing out 'school dinners' was a stark reminder of the numbers of children that depend on schools to provide basic nutrition. Writing in the *Lancet Child and Adolescent Health* in April[12], a team of researchers based at the UCL Great Ormond Street Institute of Child Health, at University College London, argued that policymakers should weigh up the harms caused by school closures against the benefits, with a view to reopening schools at the earliest opportunity. The team noted that 'the scale and speed of school closures are unprecedented globally', yet there is limited evidence about the positive impact of this in limiting the spread of an infection such as Covid-19. On the other hand, school closures have some clear 'adverse effects', including:

[E]conomic harms to working parents, healthcare workers, and other key workers being forced from work to childcare, and to society due to loss of parental productivity, transmission from children to vulnerable grandparents, loss of education, harms to child welfare, particularly among the most vulnerable pupils, and nutritional problems, especially to children for whom free school meals are an important source of nutrition.

Many others worried about the impact of locking children down with parents who might be abusive, to their children or to each other, outside of the everyday purview of the school. Others, less dramatically, drew attention to the negative effects on children's social and emotional development of being isolated for some time from adults or children outside of their immediate family.

Lockdown has meant that children have been thrown back onto the care and resources of their parents at a startling speed, and at a time of immense pressure, with parents expected simultaneously to work from home and supervise their children's schoolwork, or to shoulder the consequences of a sudden loss of livelihood. In practical terms, this will have terrible consequences for some families, including poverty, abuse, and educational failure. We should also acknowledge that the effects of lockdown for most families will be more mixed, and that they will ride out the problems in the same way that they have had to ride out the many other misfortunes of life in the time Before Corona.

But again, the question for generational consciousness is the symbolic impact of this moment, which will reverberate through all families. With the closure of schools, young people experienced the retreat of adults' general sense of care and responsibility. Shut up in their homes, they have been subjected to the sole authority of their parents, yet with their parents having a very weak authority in practice. Many of the daily decisions that parents make about what their teenagers could do – who to see, where to go, what time to be home – were taken out of their hands by the legal requirement to 'stay at home'. This may have reduced some of the daily conflict but gives an uneasy sense of who is in charge.

Parents' authority, and teenagers' burgeoning desire for independence, have both been compromised by the absence of privacy afforded by the 'Stay Home' injunction. With their interactions with peers and school reduced to anything they could do online, teenagers have had to conduct their intimate conversations in the knowledge that they could be monitored or overheard. Conflicts between parents, online meetings with work colleagues, and the sensitive discussions that might normally be had 'not in front of the children' – have had to play out in the theatre of the entire household.

If anything, this became more fraught as lockdown measures began to ease. Young people were cast out of the public world, but any physical interactions had to take place in public space – putting them under a state of constant surveillance, not least by those members of the community quick to jump on and report teenagers as rule-flouting 'Covidiots'. Teenagers have had to navigate parents' different interpretations of the rules, putting them in an invidious position of balancing the 'rightness' of their own parents' approach with that of their friends' parents.

How much of a problem is this? Understanding that the adult world is flawed and contradictory is all part of growing up; without it, we would never have had all those books and films dealing with the pain and promise of coming of age. Society will move beyond lockdown, and the Corona Generation will find its path, as others have before it. But as adults, we should acknowledge our own responsibility for shaping that path in the direction of an open future, rather than a grim dead end.

Emma's lockdown reflections: Learning uncertainty

Although the initial reactions to the cancellation of exams differed, there was a shared view that it was the only way forward in the circumstances, as the anxiety caused by the wave of uncertainty was overwhelming. Nevertheless, the limbo in the beginning unnerved so many people and I think a lot of us took weeks to recover from the pure speed at which the whole situation took off. Despite many GCSE students being relieved from huge pressure, the closure of schools and exams was not so good for others, especially for those in a period of transition. Sixth formers applying to university were unsure of how the application process would work, yet another instability in an already uncertain time; and those about to go to university had a massively strange experience, with the cancellation of one milestone yet still being expected to prepare for this massive turn in their lives. A-level students have also been stripped of the newfound independence of moving away from parents into the unknown, becoming more stuck at home than they have been for years before.

There are many difficulties brought with uncertainty, as in the lockdown there is no direction, not only for young people but those they look up to. There is a huge lack of direction and purpose at a time when we need it the most, a time we are supposed to find our feet and independence. This was bigger for many people than the act of cancelling exams, as what really worried them was the destabilization of society and its processes around them; education is struggling to move forward, there is a focus on grades with no exams, and lessons with no teacher. The structure and direction of education is gone, with no timetable or teachers to correct your mistakes.

This creates a very testing time, as it requires much higher motivation levels and self-discipline. For many this is massively unfair due to disadvantages at home, with different pressures and family struggles, but this could be seen as a more accurate test of skill and self-control for the next year of exams, as the students who have managed to push themselves through the spring and summer months will show. This will highlight what an impact the teaching at schools really has, and why the exams may not be as accurate as they are said to be, because in a lot of cases it will tell you more about the school and its area than the student.

There are added complications for families and providers in the more disadvantaged areas. There are difficulties with trying to teach those children who have a lack of support and discipline at home, or are crowded or hungry. There are priorities of the students' fundamental safety which takes over from the education; this has been highlighted by the pandemic as these schools have been desperately trying to provide some sort of support for these families, especially seen through packages to help with food shortages, along with the fundamental education.

This further emphasizes the inequality in education as some children don't have any access to online schooling and therefore have a lack of contact with the school, meaning they will entirely miss out on the next months of school gaining a further academic disadvantage. Adding to this there are problems seen with disruption which tend to appear after the holidays, therefore the fear yet expectation from teachers is that the lack of discipline and regard for education by parents will result in a lack of focus when school returns. The lockdown will not only disadvantage students' current academic progress, but also in the following months; as they have come to adapt to different lifestyles, they may become even more heavily unmotivated.

This can also be said for the shift of education into the family. How can you expect children to learn without direction and guidance? Children at home have very different approaches to studies and limited resources. You cannot push and encourage them in the same way as at school and neither can their parents. The role of education, but especially teachers, is to allow children to discover, with some autonomy but also guidance to stay on track. Teachers are equipped with the attention, records, and understanding to do this. However, at home this is lacking; parents at home are working and still need to provide income, so there is no extra support. The focus in the home is not on the children, so will they stay on track? Some may but many won't. Aside from this many parents are unaware of the education system and its vitalities; as different authorities don't push education in a coherent manner parents won't have the same knowledge and will have different reactions to the closure of schools, therefore the fundamentals will crack and education will change. And how will its importance be restored after a long period of semi-structured 'lesson time'?

The current education process is really going to be put into question after these events; as we have become so accustomed to the exam style, teacher dependent learning, the sudden shock to the system questions the fundamentals in many ways. To many students nationally the hasty decision to cancel these exams was not only a shock to their future but to the fundamentals of their education, where they had been drilled into learning the textbook. This leads us to question whether there is a better way of doing things as we are now separated from our exams and courses. Is there a system which allows for more freedom, experimentation, deeper development of skills for the workplace?

Furthermore, not only has it shaken the fundamentals of education but really emphasized the importance of globalization, and therefore it may be that a new reform is needed, with an added emphasis on business and international trade, moving away from such a focus on trigonometry and Shakespeare. However, there are many fundamentals to education, so I am not arguing that it needs to undergo a massive renovation in what the subjects teach but the ideas behind them, as surely we should be studying Macbeth for the analysis of the depiction of relationships and stereotypes at the time, rather than a certificate.

This is often seen as a huge problem with British education, as the learning and exchange of knowledge is not valued as highly as it should be. Even those who go to great lengths to study tend to do it for the grade and the pride, rather than the knowledge itself, thus telling us lots about the individual but in the end we learn very little about the subject because in reality we are required to learn through intense cramming, rather than deep and retained understanding. The time many of us have been given allows for a freer style of learning, whether people take it or not, giving us a chance to explore the subjects we love and enjoy rather than for the alternative. This is a refreshing insight into the meaning of education in a much more competitive environment.

The massive increase in online education could either change our education for better or worse, as already the introduction of computers into the classroom has allowed for more independence and alternative education, but now with it being more available will we be asked and expected to be more autonomous? Will there still be the monotony of textbook exercises? Or will there be a wider and more individual curriculum?

Chapter 5

Lockdown labelling

On 27 March 2020, a pair of twins were born in the Indian state of Chhattisgarh. Their parents named them Corona and Covid. 'The delivery happened after facing several difficulties and therefore, my husband and I wanted to make the day memorable,' the twins' mother told news agency Press Trust of India. 'When the hospital staff also started calling the babies Corona and Covid, we finally decided to name them after the pandemic.'[1]

With luck, most babies born in the spring of 2020 will escape the fate of being literally named after a virus – but commentators are already competing for the most dramatic ways to claim that their lives will be scripted by the pandemic. Jordan Patel, a 'social entrepreneur' writing on Euronews, lists a string of horrific consequences for the kids of today. He warns of an increase in online bullying, suicide, and misery, compounded by 'the increased stress of constantly being at home, the general atmosphere of uncertainty and panic as the pandemic worsens and parents too busy taking conference calls to notice their child's despair'. Final year university students 'will graduate (without ceremonies) into an unstable world of work', competing in a market where 'there may not be enough space for everyone'. All in all, Patel predicts that 'the coronavirus has the potential to create a generation of socially-awkward, insecure, unemployed young people'.[2]

Writing in *The Atlantic,* Amanda Mill picks up on a colleague's suggestion that 'babies born in the post-coronavirus era, who will never know life before whatever enduring changes lie ahead, might be called Generation C'. She argues that this generation 'includes more than just babies':

Kids, college students, and those in their first post-graduation jobs are also uniquely vulnerable to short-term catastrophe. Recent history tells us that the people in this group could see their careers derailed, finances shattered, and social lives upended. Predicting the future is a fool's errand even when the world isn't weathering what looks to be an epoch-defining calamity, but in the disasters of the past lie clues that can begin to answer a question vital to the lives of millions of Americans: What will become of Generation C?[3]

The question 'what will become of our kids?' has become rhetorical, with the answer in the negative. As we emerge from lockdown, we can expect much breast-beating about the terrible fate that this virus has determined for our young people, who will enter a labour market framed by high unemployment, low pay, and levels of public debt that make the previously-existing mountains appear like molehills. If we are not very careful, politicians will excuse all this as the result of something that 'had to be done' to protect society from a disease that mainly ravages older people, and leaves young people relatively unaffected. The underlying economic, social, and cultural problems that were already shaping the life chances of 'Generation Z' will be airbrushed from their story by the global claim that 'the virus made us do it', and that young people will just have to shoulder the burden of whatever comes down the line.

Will the young put up with it, or will they fight back? Will they resent us for hobbling their freedom, or thank us for saving the world from a terrible disease? Commentators will be asking all these questions, and in time we might have an answer. For now, what young people need from us most are clear heads and open minds. While we should acknowledge the impact that this crisis has had on their present, we will do them no favours by imagining that it will determine their future.

Big problems, little stories

At a cultural level, the Covid-19 crisis has played out as a tale of two cities. In Working from Home-City, the professional or corporate executive glories in the lack of commute and the lovely long walks and bike rides, spending time baking with their children in the gaps between their enriching Zoom lessons, put on by private schools desperate to justify the fees. The citizens of Working From Home-City boast about how much money they are saving by making their own lunch, and pontificate about how much we can benefit from this slower, less consumerist lifestyle, as they wait impatiently for their next online delivery from a driver who doesn't even require a tip, thanks to social distancing rules.

Meanwhile, the population of Keeping Things Going-City make their way to work in supermarkets, care homes, and waste disposal services, using whatever limited form of transport is currently available. These 'essential workers' – often in low-paid work and disproportionately from ethnic minority groups – are rhetorically applauded and wept over in the grim daily 'Covid-19 death' tally, but they are otherwise invisible. These are the people who will bear the brunt of health effects of the virus, economic effects of lockdown, and educational effects of school closures.

In other words – the big story of the Covid-19 crisis will turn out to be one of class, not generation. And even here, people's real lives do not simply reflect the crude cultural binary imagined by the tale of two cities: individuals' experiences of lockdown have also been affected by where they live, whether they have families depending on or caring for them, whether they are enjoying a leisurely break 'on furlough' or desperately struggling through the loss of their job.

Age does matter, particularly in the case of this virus, where the risks of serious illness are so clearly associated with advancing age. In this respect, the plight of the kettled, healthy young person is bound to be distinct from that of the fearful pensioner, bringing different anxieties and frustrations. Yet it is also true that not all young, or old, people have had the same experience as each other; hence the voices of rebellion from active, healthy over-70s who object to the idea that they should be 'shielded' for their own good[4], and the trepidation with which some young people view the end of lockdown. A major problem with blanket lockdowns is that their restrictions have ridden roughshod over the diversity of circumstances and experiences that enable people to navigate their own desires and difficulties, and tolerate or empathize with others taking a different approach.

It should also be stressed that the Covid-19 crisis, for all its unprecedented character, has not brought in a raft of new problems, so much as accelerated those that were already there. Particularly at the beginning of lockdown, the difference between 'normal' life and 'Covid' life seemed very stark, throwing into question the norms and assumptions that had underpinned social life to date. The demand not to visit elderly parents, hug our friends, go out to work or send our children to school felt like a shattering of all the established rules about how good people and citizens should behave. Yet at the same time, these demands seemed to reflect trends that were already embedded in social and cultural life.

Widening social and economic inequalities, social atomization, and the decline of trust have long been discussed as features of late modern capitalism. Even before the global economy came crashing down, the prospects for school and university leavers were widely acknowledged to be inauspicious. Since the 2007/8 global financial crisis, a combination of low wages, high house prices, and insecure employment contracts have provoked concerns about social mobility and 'fear of falling'.[5] This crisis is shedding light on an already-apparent schism between the role played by educational credentials in securing a 'good job', and the kind of work promoted by the 'knowledge economy'.

For those kids not inclined towards graduate careers, who were previously funnelled into work through apprenticeships and vocational courses, social distancing requirements and tightening labour markets are likely to restrict those opportunities in the short term. To the extent that the pandemic provokes a shake-down of the economy, enabling an eventual return to greater investment and productivity, the economic future may at some point be dynamic rather than dystopian. But in the short term, young workers-to-be will be forced into an intense re-think of their career ambitions and expectations.

And that's just in the wealthier nations. The implications for what is now fashionably, euphemistically described as the 'Global South' seem particularly grim. On 29 April, the International Labour Organization (ILO) warned that 'the continued sharp decline in working hours globally due to the COVID-19 outbreak means that 1.6 billion workers in the informal economy – that is nearly half of the global workforce – stand in immediate danger of having their livelihoods destroyed'. 'For millions of workers, no income means no food, no security and no future. Millions of businesses around the world are barely breathing,' said ILO Director General Guy Ryder. 'They have no savings or access to credit. These are the real faces of the world of work.'[6]

These problems seem so huge and overwhelming that it would be reasonable to ask, who cares what a few kids think about the impact on their own futures? What can their little stories, about lives that have barely begun, tell us about the crisis that gripped the globe in 2020? Maybe not a lot – but certainly enough that we should be listening.

The fatalism of generationalism

Over the past few years, I have published several books relating to the sociology of generations, all of which caution against the over-use of this concept as a way of understanding social experience.[7] In recent years, media and policy discussions have increasingly deployed crass stereotypes and labels about generations ('Baby Boomers', 'Millennials', 'Generation Z') to make simplified claims about the outlook and experience of hugely diverse age cohorts. This has resulted in the rise of generationalism – where social, economic, and political problems are presented through the distorting prism of simplified generational differences.[8]

Generationalists tell us that the 'Baby Boomers' (a large cohort born between 1946 and 1965) are wealthy, powerful, and selfish – 'A Generation of Sociopaths', in the words of venture capitalist Bruce Cannon Gibney[9] – regardless of the evidence showing how Boomer fortunes, like those of any age group, are stratified by social class, ethnicity, gender, and geographical location. 'Millennials' (born in the last 2 decades of the twentieth century) are depicted either as economic and political victims of their voracious Boomer parents, or as entitled snowflakes who think avocado on toast is a basic human right.

As chatter has increased about the problem of 'entitled' Millennials, some have suggested that we should be pinning our hopes on the kids currently known as 'Generation Z'. One version of this narrative has it that the outlook of Gen Z is shaped by the pessimistic outlook of their Gen X parents, who were raised in the harsh reality of the 1970s and have allegedly brought their own kids up with a healthy dose of cynicism about what they can expect from life. The destiny for Gen Z has been imagined as grimly getting on with it – setting their horizons no higher than getting a job and fighting for survival in a pre-programmed world of cruelty and violence. 'In many ways they seem to be bracing themselves to enter a "grave new world",' wrote Rhys Blakely in the *Times* (London) in 2014:

> Ad agencies have identified the iconic Gen Z film as *The Hunger Games*, a saga in which survivalist teenagers fight to

the death in a dystopia ruled by an elite 1 per cent. Its star, Jennifer Lawrence, is the number one choice when Gen Z are asked which celebrity they'd most like to be friends with.[10]

But as Blakely points out, it is 'the world's marketers – a cabal of anthropologists, ad men and big-data crunchers' who are 'touting the idea that we're on the brink of a societal sea-change: the coming of age of Generation Z.' Others, he says, might question the assumption that our characters are 'somehow mass-produced', and that we can be 'typecast by the times we live through'.

Bobby Duffy, Chairman of the Ipsos MORI Social Research Institute and author of the 2018 report *Generation Z – Beyond Binary*, cautions that despite the fact that most of this cohort are 'still very young', Gen Z are 'the new focus of attention, and often wild speculation' – often 'the subject of spurious claims and myths about who they are and what they're going to be'. This report acknowledges that:

> They face some really tough conditions, particularly in Western countries like Britain – a tough economy, rapidly changing labour market, all-encompassing technology that brings new threats as well as opportunities, polarised politics and long-term trends like increasing obesity.[11]

But Ipsos MORI's study also highlights many 'positive aspects' of Gen Z, including 'their interest in social action and ethical consumption, their trust in others, their dropping of some past bad habits, their openness to difference on sexuality, gender and immigration'. 'Putting a whole generation into a box is never smart, but it's particularly unhelpful with this varied and fluid generation,' Duffy writes.

Duffy's comments reveal the tension at the heart of generation studies. How do we say anything about generations without subsuming all those diverse views and experiences under a simplistic script of 'what young people think'? How is it possible to distinguish an outlook that comes from simply being young to something that is distinctive to a particular generation? How is it even possible to generalize anything about being young?

Most of the time, it isn't. The journalist Chloe Combi describes how, in researching her 2015 book *Generation Z: Their Voices, Their Lives*, based on interviews with dozens of young British people born between 1995 and 2001, she was often asked how she would label the teens and young adults of today. 'Are they the Internet Generation, the Sex-Mad Generation, the Social-Media Generation, the Celebrity-Obsessed Generation or the Not-Much-To-See-Here Generation?' she asks. None of these labels fits the young people she interviewed, whose voices range from those whose lives are painfully distressing and chaotic, to others whose lives 'are so achingly normal that they worry if it rains too much'. 'There was a temptation to string together all the most shocking and affecting vignettes, but this would have been disingenuous,' Combi writes. 'The mundane is as much a feature of being a teenager as the fantastic.'[12]

But when something happens to shake the world, trying to get a handle on generational consciousness becomes both possible and important. In the wake of this pandemic, society as a whole has undergone a shock – something that has forced us to reconsider some fundamental questions to do with the relationship between health and illness, the responsibility of adults to children, and the value of physical contact. The crisis of meaning that results from this is likely to have a particular, and powerful, impact on young people because it comes to frame their entry into the adult world.

'For everyone that didn't understand the effects of 9/11, this is the most any of our lives have changed in such a short time and we will always remember that,' said Mark, 21. Mark believes that his generation will 'bounce back immediately and move on because that is what we have to do', but at the same time, 'we will not take for granted what we used to before COVID-19. We will cherish human contact; we will not take for granted being able to learn in a classroom while having the professor right there.'

Gracie, 21, sees the pandemic as confirming the unease with which they were brought up to see the future:

With the developments and the changing world growing up, with the massive growth in the marketplace, education and technology there is a wide sense of everyday growth amongst our generation. For many we were always 'on the edge of change', trying to adapt and stick with the world around us but also coping with a feeling like there was about to be a breakthrough, one that changed to form a more fast-paced, developed world, more equal and better connected. In a way the pandemic has created a sense of relief as this is the anticipated change, but due to the frequent changes and anticipation of this we as a generation feel resilient and reflexive.

Gracie talks positively about 'a shared experience which makes it easier to communicate across the globe, although they may all be very different there is a tie there'. Yet she also worries that 'the loss of time is huge, and we are never going to get that back, as well as the implications for the future – this could lead to an extended adolescence as we become more lost and it takes longer to find ourselves. But we don't know how long that will last and what we will get up to when we are out and try to complete ourselves.'

Exactly how the 'Corona generation' will work through this experience is an open question. When Mannheim theorized that a generation's sense of itself was forged by significant social events, he insisted that not all members of that generation would bring the same meaning to it. Rather, distinct 'generation units' come to represent the different ways in which members of a particular generation come to work up their experience. With the passing of time, what comes to be regarded as the voice of a generation is the voice that most clearly speaks to the *Zeitgeist*: the meaning that history comes to give to that particular moment. Shaping that history is on all of us.

As we collectively imagine the future for the 'Corona generation', we need to reckon with our responsibilities towards the young. That means facing up to the symbolic significance of what just happened: when confronted with this crisis, societies across the globe ditched the kids. We locked them in their homes, deprived them of their education, trashed their employment opportunities, and saddled them with decades of public debt.

History will debate whether this was the right thing to do in the circumstances. But even as we start the tentative steps out of lockdown, societies in North America, Continental Europe, and the UK are feeling the reverberations of uncertainty, the explosiveness of politics, and portents of the economic and social doom to come. Young people, coming to adulthood in the fractured, fearful culture blithely referred to as the 'new normal', might indeed 'bounce back' – but we should not expect them to have to do that on their own.

It is our responsibility, as adults, to have open and honest discussions with our young people about the dimensions of this crisis, and what it means for our societies going forwards. To assume that kids will be forever traumatized by lockdown would trap them in those months forever – for that reason, more than any other, we need to allow them to put all this behind them, and move on. But in doing so, let's not pretend that this experience didn't matter. Maybe we didn't mean to, or maybe we even meant well: but when the chips were down, we sacrificed our children on the altar of safety. While they might forgive us for this, we should not be too quick to let ourselves off the hook.

Emma's lockdown reflections: Politics, identity, and Generation Z

The decrease in polarization and stronger sense of political solidarity could not have come at a greater time for Britain. With the recent Brexit campaigns fracturing the country we needed a reminder of what government is supposed to mean – a sense of commitment to recovery, to realize the importance of government and its role, and I believe there has been a decline in ignorance, as we try to keep away from tensions and conflict to support the governments in the efforts to save lives. For the 'Corona generation' this is massively influential in shaping our political views, as many would have formed a preference before, but this shift in competition gives a broader sense of stability and comfort in the country as a whole. The increased engagement is also hugely influential, as young people were developing their political views they are now further engaged with the government as a system rather than as an identity campaign, increasing belief and investment in the system as a whole.

On the other hand, in many cases the government policies created through this time have come to question the democratic system, as there have been control measures and police policies rapidly put in place. Although some may see them as necessary, others disagree as people are forced under policies over which they have no control. It questions the power of government and how much we have moved forward globally in giving people full access to rights, and raises concern over how much power we have given the state, which can be used to contain people globally, showing how far many places are from a truly free and representative state.

I think this adds to a new sense of global solidarity, one which has not been seen as clearly before. Not only does it give global cohesion but it shows the impact we now have on each other through the highly commercialized world, as you can see the impact on people's employment there is an idea that you are paying someone's wages through your own, and therefore you spending your money is important in funding other lives. The hit taken by the tourism and independent industries shows the importance of the luxuries that we have developed creating new 'pointless jobs', not necessary to the fundamentals of society but necessary in other ways, providing luxuries and jobs. The difficulties facing airlines have already shown that we as a society provide so much through our expenses like holidays and this is important, as not only does it provide more diverse and extra jobs but provides relief from everyday life, which is clearly needed.

The destabilization of these jobs will further increase a growing economic divide, as while the wealthiest few are cushioned through online work, school, and the comfort of savings, the majority are likely to suffer massive instability, possible job loss, and a struggle to pay for food and bills. This highlights the growing inequalities and further shows the importance of the everyday businesses in maintaining a decent lifestyle for many more people. What worries me is the rise of those struggling across the country – with the increasing use of foodbanks it is clear that the current UK economy is not providing for those at the bottom, and this needs to be addressed as the current welfare system isn't equipped to sufficiently help those in need. It has been stated that through the course of the pandemic there has been a massive increase in the use of foodbanks, and though this is temporary it will not go down to nothing and is likely to remain higher than before; therefore many of our generation see this as a concern, especially if it continues to grow.

Government policy in the near future needs to address these issues, and the pandemic has really shown this. Not only does it increase our worry for the country as a whole but ourselves as it begs the question why so many more people are relying on foodbanks regularly and is it easier for us all to slip down that slope? It seems less avoidable than before.

The face of employment is changing: in our summer jobs and in the prioritizing of careers. In the immediate term the pandemic has aggravated many as those coming of employment age are unable to find work; the lack of jobs and funding is aggravating not only due to the lack of money in itself but also due to the removal of self-sufficiency which comes with it, as now not only are we stuck living with our parents but are reliant on them for our basics due to the removal of our personal income.

The employment market has been shown in a different light; as carers, nurses, and government are much more on centre stage, we are shown the importance of some of the more everyday (less office-based or corporate) jobs. This is very different from before the pandemic as in a world where we have been pushed into medicine or business we are now given a different emphasis and direction to prioritize which many people have overlooked. The world is becoming more globalized but what has also been shown is that there is still a huge demand for jobs in the country maintaining the care of other citizens, which is largely overlooked by education as many of the 'key worker' roles are less focused on the grades and university degree, but now the appreciation by governments has highlighted the importance and pride in this path.

Again, the increased use of the term 'key workers' in supermarkets and hospitals goes to show the fundamentals of our society, in the marketplace, in aiding the economy, and in the care of others. This is a deeper reminder of the need for social solidarity, reminding not only young people but many more that they make up a system and are more than themselves. I think this is hugely important in releasing some of the individual pressures on people and showing them they are not alone.

Politics has also become part of people's identity, with

those who simply aren't interested, and for those who are interested and favour a party, especially shown by the uprising of the Labour supporters who seem to be very concerned with equality in society. The more I got to be a part of conversations about the political parties, the more I realized that not many people seemed to question Labour's policies or views – but many were simply blindly against the Conservatives, and got rather agitated or offensive if they had found that someone would have voted for them. The turn of events leading to the closure of schools and quick-fix policies seemed to change this; people seem to have separated themselves from politics, seeing the effects of the parties and their role in government, to help and control the population rather than have a political story to tell. This to me speaks a lot about the centres of the current political priorities of young people as increasingly it is seen that they have a view which no longer highlights the importance of liberty and democracy – they want to be told what to do and where to go, with strict rules for people to follow and with more equal prospects for everyone.

For young people, the reliance on rules and regulations in politics seems strange but not surprising, as growing up in a world based on education, with strict curriculum guidelines and restrictions on going out, we are only used to being told what to do, and in a world obsessed with equality why wouldn't we enforce legislation to keep everyone the same? Yet what many seem to forget is the other effects of these changes and what that would mean, as we are still only limitedly affected by government choices and don't have full freedoms in our everyday lives, so why would we see this as necessary in the wider world, when there could be other more obvious benefits elsewhere? I think we have been tricked into only seeing the immediate effects and picture, with little control and immense protection; therefore we are struggling for safety as the world, workplace, and the economy are becoming more unclear.

Chapter 6

Moving on

Writing a book in real time presents a number of challenges – particularly when that time is as personally and politically discombobulating as 2020 has been. The book was conceived in the initial days of the UK's lockdown, when the epidemic was raging and fear was at peak intensity. Emma and I embarked on the project as a way to try to make sense of what was happening, and to work through some of the implications for the future. It is hard to be definitive when events are moving so fast and when you are working in the darkness of isolation. Although we kept telling each other that we would look back on this period from a brighter place, as the weeks dragged by it often felt as though we would never escape from the physical constraints, and the emotional disarray, of lockdown.

Now we are in July, and beginning to take tentative steps out of confinement towards what has been glibly termed a 'new normal'. Shops are opening, people are beginning to go back to work, and momentum is gathering around the need to ensure that all children go back to school in September. It is becoming at least possible to visualize a new chapter in this unfolding drama – not necessarily a happy one, given the economic catastrophe that is rapidly gathering, and the political discontent rumbling around the world. But at least things are starting to move on. When we come to reflect on the meaning of this crisis for the younger generation, we will have to take into account not only the experience of lockdown, but what happened afterwards.

For me, the question that raises its head time and again is whether we will see the emergence of a genuine conflict between the generations. In my previous work, I have drawn attention to the phoney character of the so-called 'generation wars', showing how policy and media narratives that assert a conflict of interests between old and young do not reflect the ways that people themselves think about their relations with, and responsibilities to, one another. Rather, this generationalist narrative has become a fashionable way in which political and cultural elites evade discussing, let alone confronting, the deeper social, economic, and cultural tensions that afflict our societies.

In the divisive 'generation wars' frame, the problem of sky-high housing costs, which are down to weak economies' reliance on over-inflated, financialized housing bubbles, are blamed on an ageing society in which hordes of allegedly greedy, wealthy older people have the temerity to live in their homes. The problem of high levels of public debt is blamed on the self-interested behaviour of the Baby Boomer generation, who benefited from the post-war welfare state as kids and have crippled it in retirement, having the gall to live longer than expected at great cost to health and Social Security budgets. Even contentious recent political events, such as the vote for Brexit in the UK and Trump in the US, are explained as a problem of selfish elders casting their vote against 'the future'. And so it goes on.

In the wake of lockdown, we can expect these claims to come back with a vengeance, as societies find ways to rationalize what happened, and to make people pay. Now that politicians and commentators are starting to realize the implications for young people's education and job prospects, we can expect an extension of what I have termed 'grandma-mugging' policies, which use the language of 'intergenerational fairness' to claw back money from pensioners in order to fill the black hole of public spending, and blame older people for every bad political decision that has ever happened.

If that happens, it will be a double injustice.

Old people are not to blame for Covid-19, and nor have they

benefited from the response to it. As discussed in Chapter Two, victims of this terrible disease have overwhelmingly been the very elderly. As well as being disproportionately afflicted by the ravages of the virus, older people have suffered as a result of lockdown measures. The outcry over high rates of care home deaths in the UK, New York State, and some European countries has revealed that the political focus on achieving a universal lockdown has often come at the expense of protecting the most vulnerable.[1] The demand that health services be protected from being 'overwhelmed' by critical Covid cases has presented the elderly as a burden on the system, who have a moral responsibility not to get sick. The imperative that older people should stay away from their families for months in case they contract an infection that kills them has provoked many to question the value that is given to the quality of their lives, at a time when they may not have many years or months left to them anyway.

Lockdown has been done in the name of protecting the elderly and vulnerable – but there are still big questions to be asked about whether this really was the motivation, and whether it has worked. As such, any attempt to demand reparations from Britain's pensioners on the grounds that 'we did it for you!' should be seen for what it is – another attempt to wriggle out of political accountability by putting the blame onto older generations for causing the problem in the first place.

Such an evasion would also do young people an injustice. The central problem discussed in this book is the failure of adult society to provide young people with the stability, guidance, and protection they need at a time of crisis. If we pretend that all this was necessary to prevent old people from dying, we should not be surprised by a backlash of resentment. Kids are not stupid – they know what lockdown meant for them in 2020, and what the grim 'new normal' is likely to mean for their futures.

For the past 10 years, young people have been incited to think of themselves as victims of societies organized around the needs and desires of older people. Unless we bring them into a broader discussion of the economic and political dimensions of the global response to Covid-19, and take our responsibilities to them much more seriously, we risk provoking a generation war that will be real, ugly, and destructive – all the more so because it doesn't need to play out that way.

From the start of the Covid-19 crisis, young people have shown high levels of concern about the virus and compliance with the restrictions designed to reduce its spread. Emma's characterization of her peers as 'a generation of goody two-shoes' may seem rather harsh, but it captures something that has been said about Generation Z for a long time: they are not natural-born rebels, who have set their face against the world. The signs of confusion and dissatisfaction often take a more individualized form – mental health troubles, struggles with personal identity – and this, to a large degree, reflects the problem that present-day society has in providing its young with a sense of meaning and purpose.

As lockdown dragged on, more tensions and reactions came to the fore. The Black Lives Matter protests that erupted in the US and many other countries in May and June, involving large groups of young people, seemed to reflect a number of dynamics. In Emma's interpretation, they showed an increase in political engagement that had been precipitated by the Covid-19 crisis. She writes:

While writing the book we saw a shift in how young people saw the world and related to the lives around them, as many of us became more involved, invested and excited by the news of the events globally. As the lockdown months have passed this has not faded but simply shifted focus. The Black Lives Matter campaign caused a huge spark of passion and raised the voice of the younger generations – after first hitting Instagram and then the streets, it felt like many people were really passionate about sharing solidarity with their views and trying to solve global inequalities. This was later followed by petitions to save Yemen from a humanitarian crisis, which felt less passionate and more distant, but it was still a sign of awareness of the wider world and a search for change towards equality.

In my interpretation, the protests had a more troubling dimension. They did indeed bring young people out of their homes in an expression of collective solidarity, expressing the positive sentiment that something matters more than obeying the restrictions of quarantine. But they also expressed the frustrated, disenchanted character of many contemporary forms of rage against 'the system' – a determination to force a break from the past, without a clear sense of where that change might be headed, or what might be destroyed in the process.

The speed with which the protests in the UK quickly transformed from solidarity with Black victims of police violence to a symbolic battle over statues, and performative demands for people to demonstrate their support for the protests on social media and elsewhere, seemed to indicate that this rebellion demanded its own brand of conformity of opinion and behaviour. And as with the Covid-19 crisis, adults seemed incapable of engaging with the young in a serious debate about the issues at stake, preferring either to flatter them as visionary radicals, or shame them as thoughtless, reckless 'Covidiots'.

Yet as Mannheim flagged up a century ago, a central element of the 'problem of generations' is that younger and older people have a different take on events. This can be as creative as it can be conflictual. Emma and I have certainly learnt a lot from each other in working through our differing interpretations of this crisis. I am concerned that, even if fears of an openly generational conflict prove unfounded, the prevailing ethos has managed to make both older and younger generations more self-conscious and insecure. But I also hope that Emma's more optimistic assessment of the moment will win out. She writes:

As we are coming into the summer there is less caution than anticipated as people are finding their way of adapting to the new world. Many of us are just anxious to save the summer and make up for the earthquake which has been 2020; the general feeling of precaution is modified by people's recognition of the time we have lost. However, there is less anger and resentment than there could have been; people are no longer holding onto what they have lost but trying to make the most of what they have. This has definitely shaped the way we as young people view our lives, our phones, and our place in the world, but we have not completely lost the more innocent joy for days at the beach and time spent living, not fighting to make a change. Overall I think the lockdown has shown us that we can have some choice over our lives, beliefs, and voice, but there are so many huge influences on our lives, which have now become clear to us.

Endnotes

Chapter 1

[1] Gallardo, C. (2020) 'Boris Johnson: Coronavirus "worst public health crisis for a generation"; Government steps up measures but schools stay open', *Politico*, 12 March. https://www.politico.eu/article/uk-coronavirus-boris-johnson-public-health-crisis/

[2] Pseudonyms have been used.

[3] Mills, C.W. (2000 [1959]) *The Sociological Imagination*, Oxford: Oxford University Press.

[4] White, J. (2013) 'Thinking Generations', *British Journal of Sociology*, 64(2), pp. 216-247; Purhonen, S. (2016) 'Generations on paper: Bourdieu and the critique of "generationalism"', *Social Science Information*, 55(1), pp. 94-114.

[5] Nash, L.L. (1978) 'Concepts of Existence: Greek origins of generational thought', *Daedalus*, 107 (4), pp. 1-21.

[6] Edmunds, J. and Turner, B.S. (2002a) *Generations, Culture and Society*, Buckingham and Philadelphia: Open University Press; Edmunds, J. and Turner, B. S. (2005) 'Global generations: social change in the twentieth century', *The British Journal of Sociology* 56 (4), pp. 559-577.

[7] Twenge, J. (2020) 'The coronavirus could be Generation Z's 9/11', *The Conversation*, 18 March. https://theconversation.com/the-coronavirus-could-be-generation-zs-9-11-133740

[8] Mannheim, K. (1952) *Essays on the Sociology of Knowledge*; edited by Paul Kecskemeti, London: Routledge & Kegan Paul Ltd., pp. 300-1, emphasis in original.

[9] Scott, S. (2018) *Millennials and the Moments That Made Us: A cultural history of the US from 1982-present*, Winchester and Washington: Zero Books, p. 8.

[10] Wohl, R. (1980) *The Generation of 1914*, London: Weidenfeld

& Nicolson, p. 1.

Chapter 2

[1]   AIDS: Monolith (1987) https://www.youtube.com/
      watch?v=iroty5zwOVw; AIDS: Iceberg (1987) https://www.
      youtube.com/watch?v=yVggWZuFApI

[2]   Halkitis, P.N. (2014) *The AIDS Generation: Stories of Survival
      and Resilience*, Oxford: Oxford University Press.

[3]   Moore, S.E. (2012) 'Controlling passion? A review of recent
      developments in British sex education', *Health, Risk &
      Society*, 14(1), pp. 25-40.

[4]   Castle, V. (2020) 'Queen Elizabeth's Grammar School not
      closed "at this stage" as pupils isolate over coronavirus',
      Kent Live, 13 March. https://www.kentlive.news/news/
      kent-news/queen-elizabeths-grammar-school-not-3908426

[5]   Nebehay, S. (2020) 'WHO message to youth on coronavirus:
      "You are not invincible"', *Reuters*, 20 March. https://www.
      reuters.com/article/us-health-coronavirus-who/who-
      message-to-youth-on-coronavirus-you-are-not-invincible-
      idUSKBN21733O

[6]   BBC News (2020) 'Coronavirus: Free our children from
      lockdown, says Barcelona mayor', 16 April. https://www.
      bbc.co.uk/news/world-europe-52308453

[7]   BBC News (2020) 'Coronavirus: Switzerland says young
      children can hug grandparents', 29 April. https://www.
      bbc.co.uk/news/world-europe-52470838

[8]   Flinders, M. (2020) 'Our Crisis Fatigue Crisis and the Politics
      of Coronavirus', *Social Science Space*, 8 April. https://www.
      socialsciencespace.com/2020/04/our-crisis-fatigue-crisis-
      and-the-politics-of-coronavirus/

[9]   Woudhuysen, J. (2020) 'An epidemic of doomsday
      forecasts', *spiked*, 13 April. https://www.spiked-
      online.com/2020/04/13/an-epidemic-of-doomsday-
      forecasts/?fbclid=IwAR1zIiG5Pq2y_W7KPVsNF2PAMd6B

nEEpFCS4TukQqKpXhevwj8WM-f6DOYU

[10] Scientific Advisory Group for Emergencies (2020) 'Options for increasing adherence to social distancing measures', 22 March. Emphasis in original. https://assets.publishing. service.gov.uk/government/uploads/system/uploads/ attachment_data/file/882722/25-options-for-increasing-adherence-to-social-distancing-measures-22032020.pdf

[11] See for example discussion in: Lupton, D. (1995) *The Imperative of Health: Public health and the regulated body*, Thousand Oaks: Sage; Fitzpatrick, M. (2000) *The Tyranny of Health: Doctors and the Regulation of Lifestyle*, London: Routledge; Gard, M. and Wright, J. (2005) *The Obesity Epidemic: Science, morality and ideology*, Routledge; Lee, E.J. (2008) 'Living with risk in the age of "intensive motherhood": Maternal identity and infant feeding', *Health, Risk & Society*, 10(5), pp. 467-77.

[12] Hope, C. (2020) 'Government has "terrorised" Britons into believing coronavirus will kill them, says adviser', *Daily Telegraph*, 7 May. https://www.telegraph.co.uk/ politics/2020/05/07/government-has-terrorised-britons-believing-coronavirus-will/

[13] Dixon, H. (2020) 'Government's stay at home message "too successful", leaving people "over anxious" and scared to go out', *Daily Telegraph*, 1 May. https://www.telegraph. co.uk/news/2020/05/01/governments-stay-home-message-successful-leaving-people-anxious/

[14] Triggle, N. (2020) 'Coronavirus: Is it time to free the healthy from restrictions?', *BBC News*, 7 May. https://www.bbc.co.uk/ news/health-52543692?fbclid=IwAR0RozVVUmwy1L_anu_itALFCFYBwUNihXkugF1u4bkpuFMc7xqup9roitE#

[15] Smith, G. D. and Spiegelhalter, D. (2020) 'Shielding from covid-19 should be stratified by risk', *British Medical Journal*, 369: m2063, 28 May. https://www.bmj.com/content/369/ bmj.m2063 Also see Spiegelhalter, D. (2020) 'How much

"normal" risk does Covid represent?', *Medium*, 21 March. https://medium.com/wintoncentre/how-much-normal-risk-does-covid-represent-4539118e1196

[16] Lay, K. and Calver, T. (2020) 'Under-50s less likely to die from Covid-19 than from accident or injury', *The Times* (London), 24 June. https://www.thetimes.co.uk/article/under-50s-less-likely-to-die-from-covid-19-than-from-accident-or-injury-analysis-shows-9j6323qxt

[17] Furedi, F. (2018) *How Fear Works: Culture of fear in the twenty-first century*, London: Bloomsbury Publishing.

[18] Giddens, A. (1990) *The Consequences of Modernity*, Stanford: Stanford University Press; Giddens, A. (1991) *Modernity and Self-identity: Self and society in the late modern age*, Stanford: Stanford University Press; Beck, U. (1992) *Risk Society: Towards a new modernity*, Thousand Oaks: Sage; Bauman, Z. (1991) *Modernity and Ambivalence*, Oxford: Polity; Furedi, F. (1997) *Culture of Fear: Risk taking and the morality of low expectation*, London and New York: Continuum.

[19] Guldberg, H. (2009) *Reclaiming Childhood: Freedom and play in an age of fear*, London: Routledge; Skenazy, L. (2009) *Free-Range Kids: how to raise safe, self-reliant children (without going nuts with worry)*, San Francisco: John Wiley & Sons.

Chapter 3

[1] Triggle, N. (2020) 'Coronavirus: How to understand the death toll', *BBC News*, 16 April. https://www.bbc.co.uk/news/health-51979654

[2] Reuters (2020) 'UK COVID-19 hospital death toll passes 10,000 mark, up 737', 12 April. https://www.reuters.com/article/us-health-coronavirus-britain-casualties/uk-covid-19-hospital-death-toll-passes-10000-mark-up-737-idUSKCN21U0LH; BBC News (2020) 'Coronavirus: US death toll passes 2,000 in a single day', 11 April. https://www.bbc.co.uk/news/world-us-canada-52249963

[3] Sweney, M. (2020) 'Coronavirus sparks debate over trust in media despite record audience figures', *The Guardian*, 7 May. https://www.theguardian.com/media/2020/may/07/public-trust-in-uk-journalism-eroding-amid-coronavirus-polls-suggest

[4] Cottee, S. (2020) 'The World Is Addicted to Pandemic Porn', *Foreign Policy*, 7 April. https://foreignpolicy.com/2020/04/07/coronavirus-pandemic-world-addicted-bad-news-social-media-voyeurism/

Chapter 4

[1] YouTube (2020) 'Coronavirus in UK: "We are not closing schools now" says PM', 12 March. https://www.youtube.com/watch?v=ITP3BaLY5aE

[2] World Bank (2020) 'The COVID-19 Pandemic: Shocks to Education and Policy Responses', 7 May. https://www.worldbank.org/en/topic/education/publication/the-covid19-pandemic-shocks-to-education-and-policy-responses?cid=ECR_TT_worldbank_EN_EXT

[3] BBC News (2020) 'Coronavirus: Key safeguards needed for schools to reopen – unions', 9 May. https://www.bbc.co.uk/news/uk-52596410; Turner, C. (2020) 'Parents are too scared to send their children back to school, headteachers say', *Daily Telegraph*, 7 May. https://www.telegraph.co.uk/news/2020/05/07/parents-scared-send-children-back-school-headteachers-say/

[4] Butler, K. (2020) 'Many Wealthy Parents Won't Send Kids Back to School This Fall. That's a Disaster Waiting to Happen', *Mother Jones*, 28 April. https://www.motherjones.com/politics/2020/04/many-wealthy-parents-wont-send-kids-back-to-school-this-fall-thats-a-disaster-waiting-to-happen/

[5] Munro, A.P.S. and Faust, S.N. (2020) 'Children are not COVID-19 super spreaders: time to go back to school', *Archives*

of Disease in Childhood, published online first on 5 May, doi: 10.1136/archdischild-2020-319474. https://adc.bmj.com/content/early/2020/05/19/archdischild-2020-319474

[6] Cambridge Assessment (2016) 'The average age of teachers in secondary schools', July. https://www.cambridgeassessment.org.uk/our-research/data-bytes/the-average-age-of-teachers-in-secondary-schools/; Gov.UK (2020) 'Ethnicity facts and figures: School teacher workforce', 28 January. https://www.ethnicity-facts-figures.service.gov.uk/workforce-and-business/workforce-diversity/school-teacher-workforce/latest#by-ethnicity-and-gender

[7] Hudson, L. (2020) 'Reopen the schools or a generation will bear the mental health scars; Children's Covid symptoms are usually mild, but a lack of education can be severe', *The Guardian*, 17 May. https://www.theguardian.com/global/commentisfree/2020/may/17/reopen-the-schools-or-a-generation-will-bear-the-mental-health-scars?fbclid=IwAR3Knbw6uEWSd6kvw0Hnch4mdm-DKeGqot92jAceQqBc3HP4guaW2a6TfQc

[8] Curtis, P. (2003) 'Tony Blair on education', *The Guardian*, 2 August. https://www.theguardian.com/education/2003/aug/02/schools.uk1

[9] Andrew, A., Cattan, S., Costa-Dias, M., Farquharson, C., Kraftman, L., Krutikova, S., Phimister, A. and Sevilla, A. (2020) 'Learning during the lockdown: real-time data on children's experiences during home learning', IFS Briefing Note BN288, Institute for Fiscal Studies, 18 May. https://www.ifs.org.uk/uploads/Edited_Final-BN288%20Learning%20during%20the%20lockdown.pdf

[10] Arendt, H. (2006 [1954]) 'The Crisis in Education', in *Between Past and Future: Eight Exercises in Political Thought*, London: Penguin, p. 193.

[11] Gillies, V. (2011) 'From function to competence: Engaging

with the new politics of family', *Sociological Research Online*, 16(4), pp. 109-19, paras 5.2 and 5.3. https://journals. sagepub.com/doi/full/10.5153/sro.2393

[12] Viner, R.M., Russell, S.J., Croker, H., Packer, J., Ward, J., Stansfield, C., Mytton, O., Bonell, C. and Booy, R. (2020) 'School closure and management practices during coronavirus outbreaks including COVID-19: a rapid systematic review', *The Lancet Child & Adolescent Health*, published online 6 April, 2020DOI:https://doi.org/10.1016/ S2352-4642(20)30095-X. https://www.thelancet.com/jour nals/lanchi/article/PIIS2352-4642(20)30095-X/fulltext#%20

Chapter 5

[1] Sky News (2020) 'Coronavirus: Twins born during India lockdown named "Corona and Covid"', 4 April. https:// news.sky.com/story/coronavirus-twins-born-during- india-lockdown-named-corona-and-covid-11968479

[2] Patel, J. (2020) '"Generation Corona" will miss out on life's opportunities. New creative spaces can help', *Euronews*, 3 April. https://www.euronews.com/2020/04/03/generation- corona-will-miss-out-on-life-s-opportunities-new- creative-spaces-can-help-view

[3] Mull, A. (2020) 'Generation C Has Nowhere to Turn; Recent history suggests young people could see their careers derailed, finances shattered, and social lives upended', *The Atlantic*, 13 April. https://www.theatlantic.com/health/ archive/2020/04/how-coronavirus-will-change-young- peoples-lives/609862/

[4] Ridler, F. (2020) '"I'll be the judge of what's in my best interests!": Michael Buerk and Angela Rippon lead grey celebrity revolt against shielding, declaring it is immoral and un-British to tell them what to do', *Daily Mail*, 26 April. https://www.dailymail.co.uk/news/article-8258723/ Michael-Buerk-Angela-Rippon-lead-grey-celebrity-revolt-

against-shielding.html

[5]   Ehrenreich, B. (1990) *Fear of Falling: The Inner Life of the Middle Class*, New York: Harper Perennial; Ainley, P. and Allen, M. (2013) 'Running up a Down-Escalator in the Middle of a Class Structure Gone Pear-Shaped', *Sociological Research Online*, 18(1). https://journals.sagepub.com/doi/10.5153/sro.2867

[6]   International Labour Organization (2020) 'ILO: As job losses escalate, nearly half of global workforce at risk of losing livelihoods', 29 April. https://www.ilo.org/global/about-the-ilo/newsroom/news/WCMS_743036/lang--en/index.htm

[7]   Bristow, J., Cant, S. and Chatterjee, A. (2020b) *Generational Encounters with Higher Education: The Academic–Student Relationship and the University Experience*, Bristol: Bristol University Press; Bristow, J. (2019) *Stop Mugging Grandma: The 'Generation Wars' and why Boomer Blaming Won't Solve Anything*, London: Yale University Press; Bristow, J. (2016) *The Sociology of Generations: New Directions and Challenges*, Basingstoke: Palgrave Macmillan; Bristow, J. (2015) *Baby Boomers and Generational Conflict*, Basingstoke: Palgrave Macmillan.

[8]   White, J. (2013) 'Thinking Generations', *British Journal of Sociology*, 64(2), pp. 216-47; Purhonen, S. (2016) 'Generations on paper: Bourdieu and the critique of "generationalism"', *Social Science Information*, 55(1), pp. 94-114; France, A. and Roberts, S. (2015) 'The problem of social generations: a critique of the new emerging orthodoxy in youth studies', *Journal of Youth Studies*, 18(2), pp. 215-30. Also see Roberts, S. (2020) 'COVID-19: The dangers of framing the coronavirus in generational terms', *Lens*, Monash University, 22 April. https://lens.monash.edu/2020/04/22/1380149/covid-19-the-dangers-of-framing-the-coronavirus-in-generational-terms

[9]   Gibney, B.C. (2017) *A Generation of Sociopaths: How the Baby Boomers Betrayed America*, New York: Hachette Books.

[10] Blakely, R. (2014) 'Watch out, we're Generation Z', *The Times* (London), 11 August. https://www.thetimes.co.uk/article/generation-z-teenage-rebels-with-a-cause-lbcv00n9n3d

[11] Ipsos MORI (2018) *Generation Z – Beyond Binary: new insights into the next generation*, 6 July. Press release: https://www.ipsos.com/ipsos-mori/en-uk/generation-z-beyond-binary-new-insights-next-generation Full report: https://www.ipsos.com/sites/default/files/ct/publication/documents/2018-07/ipsos-thinks-beyond-binary-lives-loves-generation-z.pdf

[12] Combi, C. (2015) *Generation Z: Their Voices, Their Lives*, London: Hutchinson.

Chapter 6

[1]   Janice Turner on coronavirus in care homes and the end of lockdown. *The Times*, 12 June 2020 https://www.thetimes.co.uk/article/janice-turner-on-coronavirus-in-care-homes-and-the-end-of-lockdown-qv9pz9z8w

CULTURE, SOCIETY & POLITICS

The modern world is at an impasse. Disasters scroll across our smartphone screens and we're invited to like, follow or upvote, but critical thinking is harder and harder to find. Rather than connecting us in common struggle and debate, the internet has sped up and deepened a long-standing process of alienation and atomization. Zer0 Books wants to work against this trend. With critical theory as our jumping off point, we aim to publish books that make our readers uncomfortable. We want to move beyond received opinions.

Zer0 Books is on the left and wants to reinvent the left. We are sick of the injustice, the suffering and the stupidity that defines both our political and cultural world, and we aim to find a new foundation for a new struggle.

If this book has helped you to clarify an idea, solve a problem or extend your knowledge, you may want to check out our online content as well. Look for Zer0 Books: Advancing Conversations in the iTunes directory and for our Zer0 Books YouTube channel.

Popular videos include:

Žižek and the Double Blackmain

The Intellectual Dark Web is a Bad Sign

Can there be an Anti-SJW Left?

Answering Jordan Peterson on Marxism

Follow us on Facebook
at https://www.facebook.com/ZeroBooks and Twitter at https://
twitter.com/Zer0Books

Bestsellers from Zer0 Books include:

Give Them An Argument
Logic for the Left
Ben Burgis
Many serious leftists have learned to distrust talk of logic. This is
a serious mistake.
Paperback: 978-1-78904-210-8 ebook: 978-1-78904-211-5

Poor but Sexy
Culture Clashes in Europe East and West
Agata Pyzik
How the East stayed East and the West stayed West.
Paperback: 978-1-78099-394-2 ebook: 978-1-78099-395-9

An Anthropology of Nothing in Particular
Martin Demant Frederiksen
A journey into the social lives of meaninglessness.
Paperback: 978-1-78535-699-5 ebook: 978-1-78535-700-8

In the Dust of This Planet
Horror of Philosophy vol. 1
Eugene Thacker
In the first of a series of three books on the Horror of Philosophy,
In the Dust of This Planet offers the genre of horror as a way of
thinking about the unthinkable.
Paperback: 978-1-84694-676-9 ebook: 978-1-78099-010-1

The End of Oulipo?
An Attempt to Exhaust a Movement
Lauren Elkin, Veronica Esposito
Paperback: 978-1-78099-655-4 ebook: 978-1-78099-656-1

Capitalist Realism
Is There No Alternative?
Mark Fisher
An analysis of the ways in which capitalism has presented itself
as the only realistic political-economic system.
Paperback: 978-1-84694-317-1 ebook: 978-1-78099-734-6

Rebel Rebel
Chris O'Leary
David Bowie: every single song. Everything you want to know,
everything you didn't know.
Paperback: 978-1-78099-244-0 ebook: 978-1-78099-713-1

Kill All Normies
Angela Nagle
Online culture wars from 4chan and Tumblr to Trump.
Paperback: 978-1- 78535-543-1 ebook: 978-1-78535-544-8

Cartographies of the Absolute
Alberto Toscano, Jeff Kinkle
An aesthetics of the economy for the twenty-first century.
Paperback: 978-1-78099-275-4 ebook: 978-1-78279-973-3

Malign Velocities
Accelerationism and Capitalism
Benjamin Noys
Long listed for the Bread and Roses Prize 2015, *Malign Velocities*
argues against the need for speed, tracking acceleration
as the symptom of the ongoing crises of capitalism.
Paperback: 978-1-78279-300-7 ebook: 978-1-78279-299-4

Meat Market
Female Flesh under Capitalism
Laurie Penny
A feminist dissection of women's bodies as the fleshy fulcrum of
capitalist cannibalism, whereby women are both consumers and
consumed.
Paperback: 978-1-84694-521-2 ebook: 978-1-84694-782-7

Babbling Corpse
Vaporwave and the Commodification of Ghosts
Grafton Tanner
Paperback: 978-1-78279-759-3 ebook: 978-1-78279-760-9

New Work New Culture
Work we want and a culture that strengthens us
Frithjoff Bergmann
A serious alternative for mankind and the planet.
Paperback: 978-1-78904-064-7 ebook: 978-1-78904-065-4

Enjoying It
Candy Crush and Capitalism
Alfie Bown
A study of enjoyment and of the enjoyment of studying. Bown
asks what enjoyment says about us and what we say about
enjoyment, and why.
Paperback: 978-1-78535-155-6 ebook: 978-1-78535-156-3

Color, Facture, Art and Design
Iona Singh
This materialist definition of fine-art develops guidelines for
architecture, design, cultural-studies and ultimately social
change.
Paperback: 978-1-78099-629-5 ebook: 978-1-78099-630-1

Neglected or Misunderstood
The Radical Feminism of Shulamith Firestone
Victoria Margree
An interrogation of issues surrounding gender, biology,
sexuality, work and technology, and the ways in which our
imaginations continue to be in thrall to ideologies of maternity
and the nuclear family.
Paperback: 978-1-78535-539-4 ebook: 978-1-78535-540-0

How to Dismantle the NHS in 10 Easy Steps (Second Edition)
Youssef El-Gingihy
The story of how your NHS was sold off and why you will have
to buy private health insurance soon. A new expanded second
edition with chapters on junior doctors' strikes and government
blueprints for US-style healthcare.
Paperback: 978-1-78904-178-1 ebook: 978-1-78904-179-8

Digesting Recipes
The Art of Culinary Notation
Susannah Worth
A recipe is an instruction, the imperative tone of the expert, but
this constraint can offer its own kind of potential. A recipe need
not be a domestic trap but might instead offer escape – something
to fantasise about or aspire to.
Paperback: 978-1-78279-860-6 ebook: 978-1-78279-859-0

Most titles are published in paperback and as an ebook.
Paperbacks are available in traditional bookshops. Both print and
ebook formats are available online.
Follow us on Facebook
at https://www.facebook.com/ZeroBooks
and Twitter at https://twitter.com/Zer0Books